CURRENT AFRICAN ISSUES 53

Sweden-Norway at the Berlin Conference 1884–85
History, national identity-making and Sweden's relations with Africa

David Nilsson

NORDISKA AFRIKAINSTITUTET, UPPSALA 2013

INDEXING TERMS:
Sweden
Africa
Foreign relations
Colonialism
International politics
Colonial history

The opinions expressed in this volume are those of the author
and do not necessarily reflect the views of Nordiska Afrikainstitutet.

Language editing: Peter Colenbrander
ISSN 0280-2171
ISBN 978-91-7106-738-8
© The author and Nordiska Afrikainstitutet 2013
Production: Byrå4
Print on demand, Lightning Source UK Ltd.

Contents

The Scramble for Africa from a Nordic perspective 5

The United Kingdoms of Sweden-Norway in the run-up to Berlin 11

The Berlin Conference from the perspective of Sweden-Norway 19

Discussion: What was Sweden doing in Berlin? 32

Conclusions: a "new" colonial past for Sweden? 41

Literature 45

Appendix 1   Transcript of document. RA: UD1902 Vol 4617a. Hochschild till Bildt 26 Nov 1884 48

Appendix 2   Translation / Interpretation by David Nilsson of appendix 1 49

Appendix 3   Transcript of letter from King Oscar to Gillis Bildt. Vol1 : Brevväxling Kungliga personer 50

Appendix 4   Transcript of letter from King Leopold II of Belgium, to Oscar II, dated 23/12/1884.
RA: UD1902, Vol 4617b 51

Appendix 3   Transcript of draft letter from King Oscar II to Leopold II of Belgium, dated 4/1/1885.
RA: UD1902, Vol 4617b 52

The Scramble for Africa from a Nordic perspective

> Congo as a state is a colonial construct, its boundaries drawn without any concern for those living there. At the Berlin Conference 1884-1885, the so called Congo Free State was given to the Belgian King Leopold II, who regarded the country as his private property. His reign of terror ceased in 1908, when the colony was taken over by the Belgian state.[1]

Few historic events have been as closely associated with European empire building and the colonisation of Africa as the Berlin conference on West Africa of 1884–85. Time after time it is reproduced in post-colonial discourses, and referred to as the epitome of Europe's political, economic and cultural domination of Africa. The quote above comes from the homepage of the Sweden's international development agency (Sida). It is just one example of how the Berlin conference is made to symbolise colonisation, European exploitation and global injustices in the past.

However, what few Swedes know – and probably even fewer people in today's Democratic Republic of Congo – is that Sweden participated in the conference and fully embraced the agreements made there. While King Leopold may have led a colonial enterprise of unmatched brutishness, all the Scandinavian countries gave him their blessing back in 1885. Of the Europeans participating in Leopold's exploitative machinery in the Congo, Swedes were the third most numerous. The many Swedish missionaries in the Congo depended on Leopold's harsh administration. Some even bought slaves to keep at the mission stations. This report aims to shed light on a dark chapter of Swedish history by exploring in detail what the united kingdoms of Sweden-Norway did – and why – at the Berlin conference. In so doing, I also wish to give impetus to a reassessment of Swedish identity in relation to Africa, including after decolonisation, and of how this identity has been constructed through historical narratives. [2]

Significance of the conference

In popular accounts, the Berlin Conference is frequently described as the occasion when the European powers divided the African continent among them-

---

1. "Kongo som stat är en kolonial konstruktion, där gränserna stakades ut utan hänsyn till dem som bodde där. Vid Berlinkonferensen 1884–1885 tillföll den så kallade Kongofristaten den belgiska kungen Leopold II som såg landet som sin privata egendom. Hans skräckvälde upphörde 1908 då kolonin togs över av den belgiska staten." From http://www.sida.se/Svenska/Lander--regioner/Afrika/Demokratiska-Republiken-Kongo/Lar-kanna-Demokratiska-Republiken-Kongo-/ accessed 2013-04-17. My translation.
2. The findings presented here form part of a research project called "Sweden and the Origins of Natural Resources Colonialism: Exploring a Small Country's Interest in the Arctic, Africa and Caucasus, 1870–1930," with funding from Vetenskapsrådet (Swedish Research Council). The project is based at the Royal Institute of Technology (KTH), division of History of Science, Technology and Environment.

selves with the help of a map and ruler. While this image is evocative and symbolically strong, for the historian it is grossly oversimplified. As Griffiths (1986) has pointed out, the straight-line geographical boundaries resulting from colonisation were not specifically agreed upon at Berlin but evolved in the two to three ensuing decades.

The conference is also widely seen as triggering the rapid colonisation of Africa in the last decades of the 19th century, the so called Scramble for Africa. However, it is a mistake to equate the conference with the commencement of colonial conquest and European domination in Africa. In his classic How Europe Underdeveloped Africa, Walter Rodney (1972) places the Scramble in a much longer context of European imperialism dating back to the transatlantic slave trade. This notwithstanding, it can still be argued that the Berlin Conference was one of the most important events in the process of European empire-building in Africa, as it laid down the international framework for the colonisation of the continent. The period prior to 1885 had seen frequent competition between the interested European powers, with mainly Britain, France and Germany competing with Portuguese and Belgian interests. With the common set of rules arising from Bismarck's negotiations in Berlin, the European powers could undertake their quest for Livingstone's "three C's" – Commerce, Christianity and Civilisation – much more vigorously (Southall 2009:5). The conference marked the starting point of the Scramble for Africa in several ways. For instance, Germany, the newcomer to global empire-building, immediately seized the opportunity to anchor new territorial claims in Africa in the Berlin Conference. Just days after the conference's ending in early March 1885, Germany proclaimed a protectorate over a vast territory in East Africa. This was based on hastily executed and legally dubious treaties between the German empire and local chiefs brought back to Bismarck the month before by German adventurer and self-proclaimed colonist Dr Carl Peters.

However, treaties with local leaders – who more often than not remained unaware of their true content – would not in the long run suffice as the sole legal basis for European colonisation. The General Act of Berlin introduced the concept of "effective occupation." For territorial claims to be legitimate, the occupier had to create some form of establishment on the ground. Consequently, one conspicuous effect of the conference and its principle of effective occupation was that the powers felt even more compelled to intervene and establish themselves on the ground. This further speeded up the scramble for colonies (Chamberlain 2010). The European powers thus soon created their own "spheres of influence" in Africa. Within a decade of the conference, writes Charles Miller (1971:169), Africa would be "arbitrarily marked up into a patchwork quilt of such spheres," a process that helped accelerate the transformation of the continent into "a chaotic conglomeration of European colonies." The principle of effective occupation laid down in Berlin, and its implementation during the rapid colonisation of Africa, were early seen as a substantial contribution to international law (de Leon 1886). They would also pave the way for an international doctrine on rules of colonisation and claim-making in other parts of the world, including remote areas such as the Arctic (Avango 2005:60). Thus, the reverberations of the meeting among a handful of white men in Berlin almost 140 years ago would extend far beyond Africa and shape social and economic global patterns for generations.

Digging up the past: is it really necessary?
Do we really need to spend time and resources on researching the past, when we are faced with so many contemporary challenges in Africa and elsewhere? Much has already been written about the Berlin Conference, and most studies of Europe's age of "New Imperialism" around the turn of the last century include an account of this event. One might think that historical studies are irrelevant to African development, or that historians should move on to other, more recent, social phenomena. However, the Berlin conference and the Scramble are indeed not closed topics. These historical processes continue to shape our understanding of the present, provide explanatory frameworks for progress and failures. For instance, Swedish institutional economists Christer Gunnarsson and Mauricio Rojas has argued that the roots of Africa's institutional crisis in the 1990s are to be found in the colonial period (Gunnarsson and Rojas 1995:258). Historical narratives can also be used as cultural tools in a wider process of legitimation and contestation regarding control over and access to African political, social and economic life.

Thus, constant interpretation and reinterpretation of history is crucial. In the case of the Berlin Conference and the Scramble, there are at least two reasons for this. First, there is still more to learn about why the Scramble took place, what actually happened in Berlin, how the actors at the time conceived of the process as well as the motives behind it. New sources and new methodologies available to historians – including electronic media – allow for new interpretations and more complete descriptions. And, as has been noted by others, reinterpreting the Scramble becomes exceedingly important in an era in which Africa is again centre stage in globalisation, and when large foreign powers are flocking to the continent. In the last decade, the world has witnessed a global surge in pursuit of natural resources, energy and food, prompting Southall and Melber (2009) to ask whether there is indeed a "New Scramble for Africa." Emerging economies such as China, India and Brazil are seeking in Africa the natural resources vital to their rapidly growing industries and are competing with the former European colonial masters to gain access to them.

There are many similarities between the old Scramble and the current aggressive appropriation of natural resources, but there are also important differences. While the Scramble of the 1800s was driven by many motives, including the need for market expansion as well as a sense of duty to civilise and convert so-called "savage" communities, today's scramble is reportedly much more focused on the extraction of natural resources such as oil, gas and precious metals. Moreover, the interaction between Africa and other parts of the world is today framed within a different geopolitical context, with exchange taking place between sovereign national states (Southall 2009). This relationship is radically different – at least at face value – from the 19th century situation described by Rodney (1972), in which the colonisers could play "the classic game of divide and conquer" merely because of "the incompleteness of the establishment of nation-states, which left the continent divided … " Nevertheless, with a neo-imperialistic world order potentially in sight, and an increasing global appetite for the resources of the South, we need to reassess the trajectories of the earlier colonisation era and learn from this part of our history.

The second reason for revisiting the Berlin Conference is that by interpreting and writing history, humans construct moral systems and world-views, that is, ways of understanding and evaluating what is going on around them. Within these world-views we shape our own identity as actors and as nations. In a broad sense, actors can seek to establish legitimacy for their agency through the historical narratives they employ. And, as pointed out by Avango, Nilsson and Roberts (2013), actors wanting to influence a region, regime or set of resources can also create legitimacy for their influence by projecting it against a vision of the future. Such visions are typically contextualised in a historical setting and, hence, will never be produced in a history-free environment. It is therefore possible to assess how actors position themselves in relation to a region by studying the historical narratives and visions of the future they construct and reproduce. In analysing Sweden's identity and position in relation to Africa, it is important to review Swedish narratives of colonisation and post-colonial futures in Africa. I contend below that Swedish history writing on the Berlin Conference – or rather the absence of such writing – has contributed to the shaping of a Swedish identity in relation to Africa, an identity that presumes Sweden lacks a colonial history in Africa. Now is the time to challenge this narrative.

The "lack" of colonial past

What were Sweden and the other Nordic countries doing during the surge of European New Imperialism in Africa from the 1880s onwards? The superficial answer has been that these countries took no part in the colonisation of Africa, and played no role at all. The fact that Sweden acquired no colonies during the Scramble has given rise to a general consensus in Sweden that the country "lacks a colonial past" in Africa. This narrative is often used, for example by the Swedish government, as justification for Swedish involvement in Africa today.

Without a colonial past burdening us as a nation, Swedish actors are seen as honest and benevolent partners and cooperation will thus flourish, the narrative goes (Öhman 2007:124ff). As Baaz has argued (2002:52), this narrative presents a "Swedish identity" constructed completely outside the history of colonialism.

However, there are reasons to question the presumption or "common knowledge" that Sweden lacks a colonial history.

Surprisingly little has been written about Sweden-Norway's role at the historic Berlin Conference and in the subsequent Scramble. The union's participation in the conference has been mentioned by international scholars and authors, including Henk Wesseling (2006) and Adam Hochschild (1998), but with no detail provided. Recently, Norwegian scholars have made important contributions to Scandinavian colonial history. A volume edited by Kjerland and Rio (2009) provides a range of accounts of the endeavours of Norwegian individuals in Africa and Asia, showing how they were part of the colonial system even if their country possessed no colonies. They were the entrepreneurs trailing in the wake of the colonialists, the "smaller brothers who did not have to plow the first furrow" but who were still able to exploit the opportunities European colonialism offered (Rio and Kjerland 2009:8). Svein Angell's chapter on the role of the union's consulates illustrates how state actors and enterprises were integrated – through trading and commercial activity – into the global colonial machinery of the late 1800s. While Kjerland and Rio's book provides important background to the Berlin negotiations and to the economic and political strategies pursued by Sweden-Norway, it offers few details about what happened in Berlin.

Very little has been written in Sweden on the topic by popular writers. The journalist Per Erik Tell has written about the scores of Scandinavians who sought their fortunes in the service of King Leopold around the turn of the last century. Among the Europeans sent to the Congo to manage the operations of the International Congo Association between 1884 and 1910, Swedes were the third most numerous, surpassed only by Belgians and Italians (Tell 2005). Tell includes a short account of the Berlin Conference, where he acknowledges the role of Sweden. However, in other popular accounts, such as that of Herman Lindqvist (1999), Sweden's departure from the former slave colony of Saint-Barthelemy in 1878 is portrayed as the definite end to Swedish colonialism.

Academic historians have also skirted the role of Sweden-Norway at the Berlin conference. In Norstedt's ambitious series on the history of Sweden, historian Bo Stråth writes about the Swedes working in the Congo and their role in the colonial exploitation of resources and people. By way of background, he also alludes to the Berlin Conference as "a conference where, under the leadership of Bismarck, the European great powers sub-divided Africa with the use of a ruler" (Stråth 2012:478, my translation). Not mentioned is the fact that the united kingdoms of Sweden-Norway were officially represented in Berlin by the king's envoy Gillis Bildt, and that they endorsed the rules of colonisation laid down in the General Act of the conference. Furthermore, from the "Berlin Conference" entry in the main Swedish encyclopaedia – Nationalencyklopedin – you will learn about the conference and its significance for the partition of Africa, but both its 1990 and 2009 editions refer to the participants only as the "leading European powers and the USA."

The only previous in-depth study of Sweden's role at the Berlin conference is to be found in Carl Yngfalk's unpublished master's thesis.[3] In it, Yngfalk concludes that the Swedish foreign ministry mainly sought to secure future Swedish trade interests, but also wished to reinforce political bonds with Germany. Although this study overlooks the role of King Oscar, and downplays other possible motives for Sweden-Norway's participation in Berlin and the Scramble, it contributes important findings based on archival research, not least about how the conference was portrayed in the main Swedish newspapers of the time.

The current report seeks to fill a gap in Swedish and African history writing by describing in detail what occurred in Berlin from Sweden's viewpoint. Based on in-depth studies of archival documents, it sets out to describe what Sweden did at the conference; who the main Swedish actors were and what their objectives and interests were; as well as Sweden's role in the greater play in Berlin and beyond. I also wish to provide an empirically based starting point for discussing how history and narratives are used as cultural tools in national identity and self-images of Swedish and Nordic relationships with African societies, and to legitimate claims and promote geopolitical interests both in the 1880s and today.

I start by presenting an overview of Sweden-Norway's foreign policy at the time, which is necessary for understanding how and why the union did what it did at the conference. I also describe the background to the conference and introduce the key Swedish actors. Then, I relate the story of the Berlin conference in chronological order from the perspective of key Swedish actors, based on the traces left in the Swedish archives. Thereafter, I discuss possible motives for Sweden-Norway's involvement in Berlin and beyond. Finally, I discuss the findings and the narrative presented in preceding section.

---

3. Yngfalk, Carl. Sverige och den Europeiska kolonialpolitiken i Afrika. En studie av utrikesministeriets och opinionens bemötande av Berlinkonferensen 1884-85 och Kongofrågan 1903. D-uppsats. Historiska Institutionen, Stockholms Universitet, 2005 (unpublished).

The United Kingdoms of Sweden-Norway in the run-up to Berlin

Sweden-Norway's foreign relations in 1884

Sweden had acquired Norway by force and through negotiations with Denmark back in 1814, as an outcome of her involvement in the Napoleonic wars. Sweden had lost Finland to Russia five years earlier, and the union with Norway was seen as compensation, or a second best alternative. A sense of lost pride and a longing for the former glory of the Swedish empire around the Baltic Sea permeated Swedish foreign policy for much of the 19th century (Lindberg 1958). The desire to recapture Finland from Russia was an important factor in Swedish foreign policy right up to the Crimean war of the 1850s. Throughout this period, Sweden manoeuvred between the two great European powers, Great Britain and France, to rally support for this cause, however, without success. As a proxy for empire, between 1814 and 1870 Sweden sought to strengthen cooperation among the Scandinavian countries, a policy doctrine known as *Skandinavism*. This led to – among other things – a Scandinavian monetary union and a joint postal service (Stråth 2005:198ff).

Sweden-Norway had a marginal but fairly well balanced position in the European power game and economy. The kingdoms enjoyed substantial trade with all the main powers during the 1800s. Although Sweden-Norway had taken a neutral stance in European conflicts after 1814, there was heavy reliance on France and Britain as guardians of the peace through a security treaty – the so called *Novembertraktaten* – of 1855 (Johansson and Norman 1985). This was meant to provide security backing for the militarily weak kingdoms against Sweden's arch-enemy Russia. The unification of Germany under the leadership of Chancellor Bismarck in 1870, and the German military victory over France in 1871, however, changed the power game completely. France was no longer the brightest star on the continent and the old security arrangements were of little value. From this point on – and particularly with the accession of Oscar II to the Swedish throne in 1872 – Sweden made its allegiances clear: it would create stronger ties with Germany (Lindberg 1958).

Constitutionally, the foreign relations of Sweden-Norway in 1884 were a one-man show. The Swedish constitution of 1809 gave the king the sole right to decide in relations with foreign powers, including the signing of international treaties and declaring war. While virtually all other government business had to be decided in the ministerial council, the king had full discretion to decide upon any matter prepared by the minister for foreign affairs. There were checks and balances: the King could not decide on the kingdom's finances, meaning that for any intervention abroad that would cost money, he needed the backing of the finance minister and the ministerial council. Although Norway enjoyed limited self-rule, the constitutional disposition of foreign affairs meant the

Norwegian government had no formal say in the foreign affairs of the union (Stråth 2005).

The Norwegian government's limited influence on matters of interest to both countries was one of the bones of contention in relations between Sweden and Norway at the time. The Norwegians wanted more independence, and also to have an influence on foreign policy. During the spring of 1884, King Oscar got involved in a bitter struggle with Norwegian civic leaders, who wanted constitutional change for more self-governance. The king considered many drastic solutions to the union's crisis during the spring of 1884, including abdication and a coup d'état. He also sought support from Chancellor Bismarck for military intervention, but Bismarck was cold about this idea. In the end, the king yielded and a revised constitution was passed that would soon reduce the king's power, including his influence over foreign affairs (Stråth 2005:259ff).

Rune Pär Olofsson, in his book on Oscar II, describes 1884 as "one of the most miserable years" for the king. Not only did he have to cede some of his power in governing Norway, but he also had problems with mistresses, and public anti-royalist sentiments were fanned by much debated court proceedings against the writer August Strindberg in the fall of 1884 (Olofsson 1985). When a telegram to the king – who at the time was in Christiania, now Oslo – arrived on 20 October 1884 from the foreign ministry in Stockholm regarding the official invitation to a conference in Berlin, it perhaps came as a welcome relief. In the telegram, the minister for foreign affairs, Count Hochschild, asked if he could announce his majesty's acceptance. Oscar replied the same day: "With delight. I presume Bildt will have the assignment."[4]

And so all three key Swedish actors in the Berlin drama have been introduced: King Oscar II; Carl Hochschild; and the Swedish envoy in Berlin, Gillis Bildt. To understand better the Swedish part in the negotiations in Berlin, short biographies of each are called for.

The actors: a king and his knights

Oscar – born in 1829 – succeeded his brother Carl in 1872 and is often described as an active ruler, showing great interest in both domestic and foreign policy (Lindberg 1958, Svenskt Biografiskt Lexikon – SBL).

Oscar became personally involved in government affairs, and was a keen writer of letters, memoirs as well as poetry (SBL). His broad interest in the running of the kingdom is reflected in his posthumously published memoirs, consisting of three thick volumes; one devoted to domestic affairs, the second to the union and the last to foreign affairs (Oscar 1960-62). He was intent on protecting the monarchy, which he felt was threatened by a surge of republican-

---

4. "Mycket gerna. Jag förutsätter att Bildt får uppdraget. Oscar." Kung Oscar till Utrikesministern, 20 Okt 1884. RA: UD1902, Vol 4617a.

Figure 1. Oscar II, King of Sweden 1872–1907 and King of Norway until 1905.
Image Source: Jacobsson, Selma, Porträtt av Oskar II, Kungliga Biblioteket, KoB Fb.17.

ism throughout Europe. "Social republicanism," according to Oscar, was "the disease of this century" (Lindberg 1958:32).

Rune Pär Olofsson (1985) describes Oscar as energetic and extroverted, as well as cunning and calculating, although sometimes indecisive. Stråth for his

Figure 2. Carl F.L. Hochschild, Minister for Foreign Affairs 1880–85.
Image source: photographer unknown, Porträtt av Carl F. L. Hochschild, Kungliga Biblioteket, KoB Sn.5.

part compares Oscar II with his predecessor Carl, and finds him more idealistic and more burdened by his sense of duty (Stråth 2005:249). Thanks to his social skills and energy, he had a wide network among the ruling elite Europe, something he was keen to use in pursuing his and Sweden's interests in Europe. He wanted a role in the larger power politics, but as the historian Folke Lindberg expresses it, "at times ... found it difficult to satisfy his lust for foreign politics within the narrow frame assigned to him as the ruler of a small country" (Lindberg 1958:27f, my translation). At an early stage, he came to regard the newly unified German Empire under the leadership of Bismarck – whom he admired – and Kaiser Wilhelm as an important bulwark against radicalism and

Figure 3. Gillis D.A. Bildt, Swedish envoy in Berlin 1874–86 and prime minister 1888–89.
Image source: photographer unknown, Porträtt av Gillis D.A. Bildt, Kungliga Biblioteket, KoB AB.1.

republicanism in Europe. Oscar's desire to build strong ties with Germany from the 1870s onwards was not just about politics and economics, but also had to do with protecting the *ancien régime* against socialists and republicans (Stråth 2005:284).

Although the king enjoyed sole discretion over foreign affairs until 1885, he still depended on the machinery of the ministry for foreign affairs, presided over by the minister. Carl Fredrik Lotharius Hochschild was born in 1831 to a knighted diplomat. By the time he was appointed minister for foreign affairs in 1880, he had a long career as a senior diplomat behind him, involving postings to Turin, Berlin, London and other places in Europe. In the otherwise conservative circles of the diplomatic corps, Hochschild was known to support reforms and have relatively liberal ideas. His opinion of Bismarck was much less positive than Oscar's and he is said to have referred to the chancellor as "this pseudo-great man" (SBL). His relationship with King Oscar was never very good, with the latter labelling him a "German-hater" (Lindberg 1958). This relationship deteriorated further as a result of Hochschild's liberal stance during the union crisis of 1884. In 1885, Hochschild was forced to resign his post and became the first chairman of the Swedish Export Association, the predecessor of the Swedish Trade Council (SBL).

Gillis Didrik Anders Bildt was born into the Swedish nobility in 1820 and during a successful career in the military met and developed a good relationship with Crown Prince Carl (Oscar's elder brother). Bildt held several influential positions as a government official before being appointed minister in Berlin and his majesty's envoy to the Prussian court and Germany in 1874 (SBL). As can be seen from the copies of his correspondence in the archives, Bildt enjoyed the trust of and an unusually close relationship with both Carl XV and Oscar II, as well as many other high potentates in Sweden (Linde 2004). Although Bildt himself was hesitant about the appointment to Berlin, Oscar was confident he would be the right person to improve relations with Germany. He is said to have developed a good rapport with Bismarck, as a sign whereof he was awarded the Order of the Black Eagle. Oscar suggested in 1880 that Bildt be appointed minister for foreign affairs, but Bildt declined the offer, and the appointment went to Hochschild (Lindberg 1958). After Bildt returned home from Berlin in 1886, he was appointed marshal of the realm – the highest official position at the royal court – and then Swedish prime minister in 1888-89 (SBL).

Preparing the table in Berlin

The process leading up to the Berlin conference, and hence Oscar's enthusiastic telegram from Christiania of October 1884, has been extensively covered by other scholars and writers. What follows is a condensed overview.

When the conference was called, many European powers had an interest in West Africa. While some had centuries-old relations with this part of the continent, others had just begun to show an interest in Africa. The once great naval power Portugal claimed sovereignty over the coastal areas of the Congo, claims dating back to its glory days in the 16th century. Britain also had long-standing trade interests in West Africa. After the slave trade was abolished in 1807, British interests were focused on palm oil mainly from the Niger basin. In return, British producers found a new export market for textiles, firearms, spirits and hardware. France, for its part, having suffered humiliating defeat at the hands of Germany in 1871, sought to restore some of its lost national pride by pursuing an active colonisation policy in West Africa. It thus soon became a fierce competitor to Britain in the region (Chamberlain 2010). The Netherlands also had interests to protect in West Africa. A Dutch trading and manufacturing company had been established in the Congo as early as 1858, and Dutch businessmen would dominate trade on the Congo for decades (Wesseling 1981).

From the 1870s, King Leopold II of Belgium assumed a particularly influential role in the international politics affecting the Congo, and consequently in setting the stage for Berlin. Leopold personally felt very strongly about the idea of creating a Belgian colony. After failing to secure political support from the Belgian government for colonial adventures, he took the quest upon himself. Ever since the 1860s, he had been exploring different options for acquiring a colony, including buying the Philippines from Spain. While he had originally envisaged a territory in the East Indies, over time his interest was increasingly drawn to Africa. In September 1876, Leopold arranged a conference in Brussels of distinguished geographers, scientists and explorers from Europe. The subject of the conference, said Leopold in his opening speech, was one of the greatest facing humankind – opening up Central Africa to civilisation (Wesseling 2006:89ff). But Leopold's motives would later prove to be more crass. After the conference, and away from grand philanthropic gestures and the pomp of scientific conferences, Leopold wrote to his ambassador in London: "I do not want to miss a good chance of getting us a slice of this magnificent African cake" (Roeykens 1955 cited in Pakenham 1991:22).

Leopold's conference in Brussels laid the groundwork for the first of a series of organisations – all forming part of Leopold's colonisation endeavour – known as the International African Association. In 1878, Leopold then formed the Comité d'Etudes du Haut-Congo, nominally a research society for the upper Congo. To garner fame and publicity for his project, in 1879 the King hired Henry Morton Stanley – the journalist cum explorer cum adventurer who had found the supposedly lost missionary Dr David Livingstone – as his main representative in the Congo. In 1882, the two first associations were succeeded by a third and longer-lasting, the International Congo Association. Throughout, Leopold managed to portray himself as a philanthropist and promoter of science. However, according to Sigbert Axelsson, "it was necessary for Leopold to conceal his excessive economic interest for the region until he had acquired a tighter hold on the Congo" (Axelsson 1970:206).

Between 1882 and 1884, Leopold had Stanley draw up treaties with local chiefs around the Congo. The French were putting in place similar arrangements in their sphere of influence, namely along the north bank of Congo (Wesseling 2006:112). Leopold's activities in the Congo prompted the British to react. To curb growing competition from the Belgians and French in West Africa, Britain struck a deal with Portugal in February 1884. The UK now supported

Portuguese claims to sovereignty around the Congo. This meant that Britain and Portugal would together control all the trade on both the Niger and Congo rivers and be able to set tariffs and taxes at will, to the detriment of all other parties (Chamberlain 2010). Leopold, who had invested heavily in his Congo project, stood to lose both pride and money if the Anglo-Portuguese agreement held sway. He cunningly manoeuvred between Britain and France to convince them that there were other, more favourable solutions (Wesseling 2006:117). Faced by the turn of events in West Africa, France would soon find herself in bed with her arch-rival Germany to counter aggressive British and Portuguese diplomacy.

Germany had entered the colonialist arena later than the other great powers. Right up to 1884, Bismarck had completely opposed colonial ambitions by the *Reich*. However, matters were changing quickly. According to Pakenham (2002:201ff), there were several reasons for Bismarck's turnabout in 1884. First, through colonial expansion he wished to antagonise Britain in order to diminish the influence of pro-British forces in domestic German politics. Second, there was an increasing demand for colonies among the German public. Empire-building was regarded by many as a useful way to compensate for the economic downturn seen in Europe since the mid-1870s. German traders saw that the other European powers would soon claim the entire African continent and that the door for German entry was closing. This so-called *Torschlusspanik* prompted Bismarck to lay claims in July and August 1884 to the territory of today's Namibia and to Togo and Cameroon in West Africa. Furthermore, Bismarck wanted to ensure that German traders had free access to the Niger and Congo rivers. In August 1884, Bismarck invited the French ambassador in Berlin to his country estate, where he presented him with a proposal. Together, France and Germany would invite all the other powers to a conference, where the tricky issues of trade and sovereignty in West Africa would be settled (Pakenham 2002:212f).

The Berlin Conference from the perspective of Sweden-Norway

The account that follows builds on research carried out during 2011-13 at the Swedish National Archive in Stockholm (Riksarkivet Marieberg). Most of the documents studied are in the foreign ministry files, plus a few files containing private correspondence in the Gillis Bildt archive. The majority of documents are in Swedish, although much of the correspondence is in French, the dominant diplomatic language of the time. Where longer quotes have been translated and presented, the original quote is provided in the footnotes. Transcriptions and translations of a couple of documents of particular interest are found in the appendix. The findings to date should be seen as "work in progress," since this paper forms part of a larger research project recently begun at the Royal Institute of Technology. In coming years, more data is likely to be uncovered in Sweden and abroad, thus offering deeper insights into the Berlin Conference and the Scramble from a Nordic perspective.

An invitation to the big world

On 7 October 1884, Gillis Bildt reported from Berlin to the ministry in Stockholm that an international conference was supposedly to be held in Berlin to regulate "conditions of international law" for the colonisation of West Africa.[5] Four days later, the German government confirmed to Bildt that such a conference would be held and that Germany intended to invite the Scandinavian countries alongside an array of other European countries and *Les Grandes Puissances* (the great powers), as well as the United States.[6] Bildt, who apparently had good connections among the diplomatic corps in Berlin, informed the ministry in Stockholm the next day that all the states invited had agreed to participate, save for the United States. Bildt mused that the US was expected to "decline participation, as has happened previously in similar cases."[7] In the short term, he was proven wrong, in that the United States did indeed send a delegation to Berlin. However, he was right in assuming that the US would in the end distance itself from the process by refusing to ratify the General Act. The British position was also ambivalent from the start: the Swedish legation in London reported on 15 October that there was substantial debate in the newspapers about British participation in the conference.[8] By contrast, the king of Sweden and Norway showed no such hesitancy. When the official invitation from the German minis-

---

5. Bildt to Hochschild, 7/10/1884. RA: UD 1902, Vol 4617 a: Kongokonferensen i Berlin 1884-85 för ordnandet av handelsförhållandena i Vest-Afrika m m.
6. Not från Tyska regeringen till beskickningen i Berlin, 11/10/1884. RA: UD 1902, Vol 4617a.
7. Bildt to Hochschild, 12/10/1884. RA: UD 1902, Vol 4617a.
8. Swedish legation in London to Hochschild, 15/10/1884. RA: UD 1902, Vol 4617a.

ter in Stockholm arrived in Christiania on 20 October, King Oscar wired back his acceptance the very same day.[9]

In the ensuing weeks, the Swedish foreign ministry collected information about the issues to be discussed in Berlin and the participants' positions through the Swedish legations in Europe.[10] The stakes the invited countries had in Africa at the time differed widely, but the German minister in Stockholm confirmed that each delegation would be allowed one vote.[11] As part of the preparations, the ministry outlined the purposes of the conference – in an internal note – to be:

i. Freedom of trade on the Congo River;
ii. Implementing the Vienna Convention on freedom of navigation on the Congo and Niger Rivers, and;
iii. Determining formalities needed for new claims on African coasts to be deemed effective.[12]

The minister also informed Swedish envoy Bildt what the Swedish position would be: to ensure that Sweden and Norway enjoyed the benefits of trade on the same terms as the "most favoured nation." He explained that more elaborate instructions were superfluous, given "the relatively smaller importance of the interests we have to protect on the western coast of Africa."[13]

On 31 October, the German chargé d'affairs in Stockholm informed the Swedish government that the conference starting date was to be 15 November.[14] In the immediate run-up to this date, there was some confusion about the legal status of the delegates to be sent to Berlin. Were they really in a legal position to enter into international agreements on behalf of their countries? Bildt expressed concern about this in a communication to the ministry back in Stockholm, and asked for a power of attorney to represent the king in this specific matter.[15] Hochschild granted his request, but before the power of attorney was issued, the German chargé explained that such a document would not be neces-

---

9. German legation in Stockholm to Ministry of Foreign Affairs, 20/10/1884; Oscar to Hochschild (telegram), 20/10/1884. RA: UD 1902, Vol 4617a.
10. E.g., see PM from London 15/10, from Lisbon 18/10/1884; from Copenhagen 21/10, October 1884. RA: UD 1902, Vol 4617a
11. Draft Protocol from meeting with the German minister in Stockholm, 28/10/1884. RA: UD 1902, Vol 4617a
12. "Fastställande av de formaliteter som böra iakttagas för att nya besittningar å Afrikas kuster må anses såsom effektiva." P.T. ang Kongokonferensen, 25/10/1884. RA: UD 1902, Vol 4617a
13. "Den jämförelsevis mindre betydelse de intressen hvilka vi hafva att tillvarataga på Afrikas vestra kust gör en i detalj gående instruktion för de Förenade Rikenas ombud i konferensen öfverflödig." Hochschild to Bildt (koncept), 25/10/1884. RA: UD 1902, Vol 4617a.
14. Hochschild to Bildt, 31/10/1884. RA: UD 1902, Vol 4617a.
15. Bildt to Hochschild, 29/10/1884. RA: UD 1902, Vol 4617a.

sary.¹⁶ However, Bildt insisted on the power of attorney. His concern was "... that the conference, despite the declaration of the German government, would find that powers of attorney are required ...," particularly since "... most of my colleagues present, including the Danish, have been furnished with powers of attorney."¹⁷ Within a few days, Hochschild had arranged a royal power of attorney for Bildt.¹⁸ And so the curtain was ready to go up on the Berlin conference on the Congo.

"Une œuvre essentiellement civilisatrice"

At 8:25pm on 15 November 1884, the ministry for foreign affairs in Stockholm received an encrypted telegram from Berlin reporting that the conference had started. During this first day, the delegates elected Chancellor von Bismarck as chairman and also decided that "until further notice the proceedings of the conference are kept secret."¹⁹ In the following days, Germany presented a proposal on the first conference item, namely free trade. If accepted as presented, the proposal would confer on Sweden-Norway equal "most favored nation" status in all trade with the region. Should that happen, concluded Bildt in his report, the issue of the highest importance (free trade) would have been resolved in "the most desirable manner."²⁰ But his optimism was premature. The next day, 19 November, Bildt had to report that the proposal had been shot down by Portugal, which insisted on its claims to sovereignty over the Congo. The United States, for its part, dismissed Portugal's claims. Hence, after only a few days the conference seemed to be bogging down over territorial claims. A smaller committee was formed, consisting of Germany, France, Britain, the US, Spain, Belgium, Portugal and Holland, to "adjust the text of the declaration," as Bildt put it.²¹

Now the detailed negotiations of the text took place between the key stakeholders in the smaller committee, and behind closed doors. Sweden-Norway and the other "back-bench" countries were regularly presented with information on the status of negotiations and the "adjusted" positions, but did not have full access to the negotiation table. For the Swedes, this provided the opportunity to work out a more precise position. In Stockholm, Hochschild drafted instructions for Bildt in which he elaborated the Swedish position, despite his earlier

---

16. Hochschild to Bildt, 5/11/1884. RA: UD 1902, Vol 4617a.
17. "...för den händelse att konferensen, oaktat Tyska regeringens förklarande, skulle vara af den mening, att fullmakter äro erforderliga"; "...de flesta av mina härvarande kollegor, bland dem äfven den danske, erhållit fullmakter."Bildt to Hochschild, 11/11/1884. RA: UD 1902, Vol 4617a.
18. Hochschild to Bildt. 17/11/1884. RA: UD 1902, Vol 4617a.
19. "Tills vidare hålles konferensens tillgöranden hemliga." Bildt to Hochschild, 15/10/1884. RA: UD 1902, Vol 4617a.
20. Bildt to Hochschild, 18/1110/1884. RA: UD 1902, Vol 4617a.
21. Bildt to Hochschild, 19/1110/1884. RA: UD 1902, Vol 4617a.

assertion that such would not be necessary. By this time, Hochschild had had the opportunity to scrutinise the draft texts under negotiation, which had been sent to him from Berlin. A handwritten copy of this four-page letter of instruction – dated 26 November 1884 – is kept in the foreign ministry files and warrants in-depth discussion. While almost all the correspondence between Bildt and Hochschild is in Swedish, this document is written in French. One may speculate that this was meant to facilitate communication of the official Swedish position to other delegates in Berlin, since French was the main diplomatic language. In short, the ministry for foreign affairs instructions to Gillis Bildt were as follows (a complete transcription is presented in the appendix).

When Sweden accepted the invitation from Berlin, it was not to seek immediate benefits in trade and navigation, but to support *"une œuvre essentiellement civilisatrice,"* essentially a work of civilisation. In Minister Hochschild's view, this work entailed spreading Christian civilisation to areas hitherto subjected to "barbarism," and it was Sweden and Norway's obligation to take part in this *"généreuse mission."* Consequently, Bildt was instructed to second any proposals that facilitated the spread of Christianity and civilisation in general. In particular, Hochschild pointed out a formulation in the draft convention text that he felt needed special attention. He noted that in the preamble, signatories resolved to take responsibility for "suppress[ing] slavery and especially the slave trade." Hochschild was concerned that if the document emphasised combating the slave trade, abolishing slavery as such would get lower priority. Hochschild therefore instructed Bildt to propose deletion of the word "especially" in order to ensure that the fight against slavery and suppression of the trade were seen as equally important.[22]

Hochschild's instruction letter dwells exclusively on the "work of civilisation," and Bildt complained the next day he lacked clear instructions on the Swedish-Norwegian position in relation to trade and commerce. These negotiations were complicated and, Bildt lamented, all he had to go by was that "the benefits on trade and navigation that accrue from decisions at the conference shall be extended also to the United Kingdoms [of Sweden-Norway] equally to those of most favoured nations." In the absence of further instructions, Bildt proposed to support "those propositions that embrace the largest freedom and the largest area" and otherwise to support "all other positions that have the approval of the German government."[23]

---

22. Hochschild to Bildt, copy of letter, 26/11/1884. RA: UD 1902, Vol 4617a. See transcription in French in appendix 1 and translation in appendix 2.
23. "de förmåner som handel och sjöfart af konferensen beslut kunna skörda [skall] tillgodokomma de förenade rikena i likhet med de mest gynnade nationer," "de förslag som afse det största område och den största frihet," "i andra frågor bör instämma uti de åsigter som af den tyska regeringen godkännes." Bildt to Hochschild, 27/1110/1884. RA: UD 1902, Vol 4617a.

Nevertheless, Bildt reported he had managed to arrange a meeting on 29 November with the commission that was still negotiating the details of the text behind closed doors. At this meeting, Bildt presented Sweden-Norway's position that "especially" be removed from the preamble of the conference document. This request fell on deaf ears in the committee. The wording had already been agreed, said the committee members, and had been introduced into the text after "careful consideration." When Bildt requested a justification, the delegates from Germany, Britain, Belgium, Spain and Portugal agreed that it would indeed be necessary to combat slavery and the slave trade simultaneously. However, the committee maintained, since slavery was "entirely embedded in African social life," it would be necessary to turn first to the suppression of the trade. The delegates built their "careful consideration" on the accounts provided by none other than Henry Morton Stanley, famous adventurer and employee of King Leopold, who had been invited to Berlin as an Africa expert.[24] Bildt also reported on a separate conversation he had had with the German delegate after meeting the committee. While Germany expressed sympathy with the Swedish position, its delegate urged Sweden-Norway not to press this issue in the plenary discussions. Bildt assured his German colleague he had no such intention and that he now felt satisfied with the information provided.[25]

The closed negotiations on the first items of the conference were slowly generating consensus, and on 1 December Bildt reported that a draft declaration had been adopted unanimously by the full conference. He noted that the free trade regime had been substantially expanded and was supposed to extend all the way across the continent to the Indian Ocean[26]. The conference, however, still had to discuss the navigation of the Congo and Niger rivers, which according to Bildt, could become contentious. [27] Five days later, a draft text regarding these items circulated among conference participants and Bildt asked for

---

24. "sade sammanstämmande att de, på grund af hvad de inhämtat rörande de afrikanska förhållandena, vore öfvertygade om det riktiga uti att nu samtidigt och med samma kraft bekämpa på en gång slafveriet och slavhandeln. Herr Stanley's fullständiga redogörelse för förhållandena i Afrika hade stadgat denna deras öfvertygelse. Han hade för Kommissionen framhållit, hurusom slafveriet är fullständigt sammanväxt med det afrikanska familjelifvet och ådagalagt, huru detta förhållande ej kan upphöra förr än slafhandeln blifvit utrotad, samt bevisat, att, om man ville uppnå målet slafveriets afskaffande – man nu först borde vända sina bemödanden mot slafhandeln, hvars afskaffande visserligen vore förenadt med stora, men icke oöfvervinnerliga svårigheter. Det var efter detta Hr. Stanleys anförande, som Kommissionen enhälligt fattade förenämnda beslut." Bildt to Hochschild, 29/11/1884. RA: UD 1902, Vol 4617a.
25. "Han tillade, att det vore mycket önskligt, att jag ej bragte denna ömtåliga fråga under ny diskussion vid Konferensens sammanträde." [Bildt svarade honom att han] "ej hade något vidare att uttala än uttryck af min tacksamhet för de fullständiga och tillfredsställande upplysningarna." ibid.
26. Bildt to Hochschild, 27/11/1884 and 1/12/1884. RA: UD 1902, Vol 4617a.
27. Bildt to Hochschild, 1/12/1884. RA: UD 1902, Vol 4617a.

instructions from the ministry with regard to it.[28] On 8 December, Hochschild assured him that Sweden-Norway could support the proposed declaration on the grounds it would not entail financial liabilities.[29] However, the assessment that the remaining negotiations would be tricky soon proved correct. Another two and a half months would elapse before the General Act of the Berlin Conference was signed. The political temperature was rising, in part because of the shift of gravity towards one key player. Now the great powers had to reckon with the monarch of one small country, King Leopold II of Belgium, and his International Congo Association.

The good brother

By December, the conference had entered a stage where the main focus was on how actually to create a framework for trade, navigation and Christian civilisation in the Congo. Bildt reported on 12 December after several days of negotiations on the navigation of the Congo and Niger rivers. The US was concerned about the neutrality of the Congo area, and in this context, Leopold's International Congo Association was beginning to take centre-stage as the presumed administrator of the Congo basin. The US wanted to turn the International Association into "a neutral Congo state." The great powers were already accepting that the writing was on the wall, and from now on Leopold's association had the upper hand. Bildt reported that Germany had signed a bilateral treaty with the association and that Britain, the US and the Netherlands were about to do likewise.[30] Within days, Bildt informed Stockholm that Britain had signed a trade and cooperation treaty with the association similar to Germany's.[31] It was rapidly becoming obvious that anyone wanting a stake in the Congo and to reap the benefits of free trade would have to strike a deal with Colonel Strauch, the secretary of the association and Leopold's righthand man. The association was ascending to a position where it appeared to be the guarantor of free trade in a neutral Congo state and the entry point for all European enterprise (Reeves 1909). However, not everyone in Berlin was happy with this, although most states were. The French delegation was uncomfortable with the emerging position of the association, and did not want to recognise it as an independent power. Bildt also expressed doubts about the feasibility of a neutral Congo state under the management of the association. In his assessment, full neutrality would place the association in an awkward position, for the simple reason that King Leopold himself had invested 25 million francs in it.[32] Whether it had the

---

28. Bildt to Hochschild 6/12/1884. RA: UD 1902, Vol 4617a.
29. Hochschild to Bildt 8/12/1884. RA: UD 1902, Vol 4617a.
30. Bildt to Hochschild, 12/12/1884. RA: UD 1902, Vol 4617a.
31. Bildt to Hochschild, 17/12/1884. RA: UD 1902, Vol 4617a.
32. Bildt to Hochschild, "enskildt," 27/12/1884. RA: UD 1902, Vol 4617a.

potential to be neutral or not, Sweden-Norway would also have to make up its mind about the association.

Thus far, the conference had delivered what Sweden-Norway had hoped for: most favoured nation status in terms of trade in the Congo. To give this effect, the kingdoms would also have to sign a treaty with the association. "This," wrote Bildt to Stockholm on 27 December, "is not of small importance to us, on the presumption that our fellow countrymen in one way or the other, have or will have, interests to protect in the Congo." He suggested that Sweden-Norway sign a convention with the association once the great powers and the Netherlands had done so. Although Sweden-Norway should not be among the first to sign, they should not be among the last either: "It is of course the Association that should approach us, but … it will not be pleasant to be last on the list …" Being an able diplomat, Bildt suggested there were ways of informally prompting the association to extend an invitation to Sweden-Norway.[33]

> Sire,
> Your Majesty, enlightened protector of scientific and civilising enterprise, allow me to inscribe you as an Honorary Member of the work we have begun to penetrate to the heart of Africa and to open this region for all nations.[34]

Thus begins the letter from King Leopold of Belgium to Oscar, dated 23 December 1884, in which he invites Sweden-Norway to enter into trade agreements with the International Congo Association (see appendix 4). As Leopold's letter predates Bildt's, it is possible the diplomat had already made his informal moves by the time he suggested them to the ministry in Stockholm. Alternatively, Sweden-Norway's potential as an ally in the Congo might already have dawned on Leopold. Leopold himself noted in his letter to Oscar that the Swedish government had already "authorised several outstanding officers from her splendid army to enter into the service of the International Congo Association. Important stations, central nodes for vast areas in the middle of Africa, are today managed by Swedes."[35]

One such "outstanding" Swedish officer was Lieutenant Matts Julius Juhlin-Dannfelt. Juhlin-Dannfelt was head of the station in Manyanga in the Congo between February 1884 and November 1884, when he fell ill and returned to Europe. Juhlin-Dannfelt would later go back to the Congo, and take on other

---

33. Bildt to Hochschild, "enskildt," 27/12/1884. RA: UD 1902, Vol 4617a.
34. "Sire, Votre Majesté, Protecteur éclairé des entreprises scientifiques et civilisatrices, a bien voulu a permettre de s'inscrire comme membre d'Honneur de l'œuvre que nous avons fondée pour pénétrer au cœur de l'Afrique et pour ouvrir cette contrée à tout les nations. » King Leopold to Oscar II, 23/12/1884. RA: UD1902, Vol 4617b : Konvention med Kongostaten.
35. "…autoriser plusieurs brillants officers de Sa belle armée à entrer au service de l'association internationale du Congo. Des stations importantes, chefs lieux des vastes districts au centre de l'Afrique, sont aujourd'hui dirigées par des Suédois. » King Leopold to Oscar II, 23/12/1884. RA: UD1902, Vol 4617b.

important roles, such as district commissioner in Matadi, as well as overseeing the construction of the Congo railways in 1888 (Tell 2005).[36] It so happens that just around the time Sweden-Norway and Leopold's Association formally made contact at the end of 1884, Juhlin-Dannfelt was in Brussels. According to the Swedish minister there, Carl Burenstam, the lieutenant was in good standing with King Leopold and with Colonel Strauch: Juhlin-Dannfelt went to the New Year's reception at the royal court in Brussels in the company of Strauch and not, the Swedish envoy noted with some concern, with himself. Burenstam went on to explain that the Swedish Lieutenant had been introduced to King Leopold at the time of his departure for the Congo a year before, and therefore his disregard of protocol could perhaps be forgiven this once.[37]

The Belgian king obviously had a particular keenness for Swedish officers in his Congo Association, an attitude said to have developed after he watched a troop of Swedish military athletes performing in Brussels in 1880. Leopold told the athletes' leader Victor Balck that they conveyed "an impression of discipline, sense of duty and strength, and that it was men with such qualities that were needed in the Congo" (Tell 2005:28, my translation). Hence, Leopold did not really need the informal nudging of the Swedish minister in Berlin to recognise the possibilities for cooperation with this other small kingdom in Europe. In his letter to Oscar, Leopold took the opportunity to thank him "for your constant benevolence towards me and the African enterprise in which I engage myself ..." Leopold closed his courteous and overwhelmingly friendly letter by signing off as "*le bon Frère, Leopold*," Leopold, the good brother.[38]

We already know that Oscar showed great interest in foreign affairs and he wanted to play an active role himself. After receiving this invitation, he seized the pen and wrote a reply on 4 January 1885, wholeheartedly accepting Leopold's proposition: "I am all the more eager to respond affirmatively to your request, as it gives me a new and welcome opportunity to support Your Majesty, whose civilising work is pursued with an admirable perseverance ..." Oscar also expressed how pleased he was with Leopold's praise of the Swedish officers, and hoped that they would demonstrate their qualities in the future as well. Oscar continued that "in serving Your Majesty, [the officers] know they serve the cause of humankind. They rejoice in doing so, and with good reason." Oscar returned the courtesies, ending his reply with "*le bon Frère*" (see appendix 5).[39]

---

36. Biographical information about Juhlin-Dannfelt in entry no.229 in the register.
37. Burenstam (Brussels) to Hochschild, 2/1/1885. RA: UD1902, Vol 4617b.
38. Leopold to Oscar, 23/12/1884. RA: UD1902, Vol 4617b.
39. "Je m'empresse d'autant plus volontiers de répondre affirmativement à cette demande dont Elle m'a honoré, que j'y trouve une occasion nouvelle et bienvenue de pouvoir être agréable à V.M., dont l'œuvre civilisatrice poursuivie par Elle avec une persévérance si admirable [...] » ; « En servant V.M. ils savent bien qu'ils servent la cause de l'humanité. Ils s'en glorifient et avec raison. », Oscar to Leopold (draft), 4/1/1885. RA: UD1902, Vol 4617b.

Thus the formalities were in place for entering into negotiations for a convention between Sweden-Norway and the International Congo Association. As there were already a number of signed conventions (UK, Germany, Spain and the US), it was more or less a matter of using these blueprints. While negotiations on the main General Act of the conference continued during January and February, several delegations – including Sweden-Norway's – were now negotiating with Colonel Strauch of the Congo Association for the signing of conventions. Sweden-Norway's proposed convention received formal blessing by the government on 12 January 1885. In a joint government sitting, which included Swedish Prime Minister Robert Themptander and his Norwegian counterpart Ole Richter, the government recommended King Oscar to conclude the convention with the association.[40] On 14 February, Bildt drily telegraphed the foreign ministry from Berlin : "The Congo convention in accordance with sent proposal signed today. Bildt."[41] The convention he signed was more or less a copy of that signed by the other states.[42] Eleven days later, Bildt reported to Stockholm that a final General Act of the conference had been tabled and had the support of all the delegations. He noted that the geographical area under the Association's control "is much larger than previously envisaged." In an almost ironic twist, in his report sent just five days before the Berlin General Act was signed on 26 February, Gillis Bildt, expressed strong doubts that European powers would seek to enlarge their colonial ambitions in Africa. The claims of Germany, Spain, Portugal and France were already well known, stated Bildt, and it was highly unlikely, he felt, that any of the powers had "any new territorial claims to stake out."[43] Almost 130 years later, this assertion may seem almost comical, considering the rapid acceleration of African colonisation immediately after the Berlin Conference. However, hindsight is the prerogative of history, not diplomacy.

Berlin General Act

I now briefly describe what it was Sweden-Norway signed up to on 26 February 1885.[44] The main purpose of the convention is described in the preamble:

> … to regulate in a spirit of good mutual understanding the conditions most favorable to the development of commerce and of civilization in certain regions

---

40. See Carl Yngfalk's study from 2005. The archival source given by Yngfalk: Ministeriellt protokoll, 12/1 1885, UD Huvudarkivet, vol 20 (A2A), Riksarkivet.
41. Bildt to Hochschild, 10/2/1885. RA: UD1902, Vol 4617b.
42. Sandgren (1905), Sveriges Traktater
43. "någon ny occupation att anförmäla." Bildt to Hochschild, 21/2/1885. RA: UD1902, Vol 4617a.
44. Based on the English version of the General Act, reprinted in the American Journal of International Law, 3, 1, Supplement: Official Documents (Jan 1909), pp. 7–25, can be found online at http://www.jstor.org/stable/2212022, accessed 18 Nov 2011.

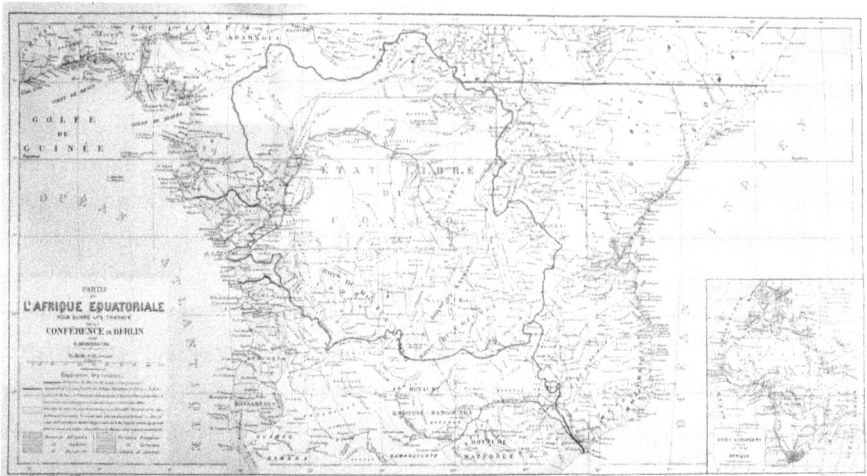

Figure 4. Map submitted to Swedish foreign ministry in 1885 outlining the geographical boundaries of the Congo state (in yellow), the free trade area under the Berlin General Act (grey contours) and the territorial claims of the European powers (coloured). Image source: Swedish National Archive. 1902 UD. 100. A/2. RA: UD 1902. Vol 4617b : Konvention med Kongo-staten. Depeche from the Swedish legation in Paris, dated 27 June 1885.

of Africa, and to assure to all peoples the advantages of free navigation upon the two principal African rivers which empty into the Atlantic ocean; desirous on the other hand to prevent misunderstandings and contentions to which the taking of new possessions on the coast of Africa may in the future give rise, and at the same time preoccupied with the means of increasing the moral and material well being of the indigenous populations …

The General Act itself is divided into six sections: i) liberty of commerce in the Congo basin; ii) suppression of slavery and slave trade; iii) neutrality of the Congo; iv and v) navigation on the Congo and Niger rivers respectively, and; vi) the rules of effective occupation.

The first section includes eight articles, ensuring the principles of free trade, protection of property and travellers, missionaries and indigenous populations, religious freedom and a common postal regime. It also defines the geographical area to which these principles apply. The boundaries of the free trade area were not confined to the Congo basin, but were extended to cover a large part of Africa south of the Sahara. In defining this area, the drafters used a combination of natural features, such as rivers and catchments, and cartographic measures. By extending the free trade area eastwards from the Congo Basin to the Indian Ocean along the 5°N line of latitude (see fig. 4), the conference set a precedent for the designation of new economic – and later political – domains in Africa by means of cartographic straight lines (Griffiths 1986).

Obviously, some sections were given less attention by the drafters than others. While section one on commercial liberty has eight articles, the second section on suppressing slavery has only one. Article 9 in the Berlin General Act affirms that:

> … the Powers who exercise or shall exercise rights of sovereignty or an influence in the territories forming the conventional basin of the Congo declare that these territories shall not serve either for a market or way of transit for the trade in slaves of any race whatever. Each of these Powers engages itself to employ all the means in its power to put an end to this commerce and to punish those who are occupied in it.

The state parties to the General Act thus agreed to a firm stance against the slave trade, but not on slavery itself. Thus, the only issue in which Sweden-Norway tried to intervene in the Berlin negotiations – fighting slavery and the slave trade with equal vigour – had been completely thrown out of the final agreement.

The section on neutrality stipulated that in case of war between any signatory powers, the territories under the free trade regime in Africa could – if the belligerent states agreed – be treated as neutral territories where no hostilities would occur and commerce could be continued.

Section four and five, on the navigation on the Congo and Niger rivers, comprised 21 articles. In principle, navigation on and access to these rivers was to be free and unrestricted for all nations. The General Act makes direct reference to a previous international convention regarding freedom of navigation, the Vienna Congress, and concludes that "these dispositions are recognized by the signatory powers as forming henceforth a part of public international law." However, while for the Niger, Great Britain was assigned the particular duty to ensure that the principles of free navigation were upheld, for the Congo it was decided to institute an International Commission of the Congo to have the same function. This commission was open to participation from all signatory powers. Apart from regulating navigation, policing, pilot and quarantine services, it would also develop lighthouses and other navigational aids, as well as supplementing river transport with railroads, routes and canals. For such investments, the commission could take out loans and charge vessels for services. Thus, while the free trade regime implied that merchants on these rivers would not be subject to duties, levies and transit taxes, they still had to pay for pilot and port services and other transport or navigation services.

The sixth section of the General Act outlined the principle of "effective occupation," which later developed into an international doctrine for the occupation of remote territories. First, all states wishing to acquire new territories were required to notify the other signatories to the Act (article 34). Secondly, for the new acquisition to be effective and legitimate, the coloniser was required to establish sufficient authority on the ground (article 35):

> The signatory Powers of the present Act recognize the obligation to assure, in the territories occupied by them, upon the coasts of the African Continent, the existence of an authority sufficient to cause acquired rights to be respected and, the case occurring, the liberty of commerce and of transit in the conditions upon which it may be stipulated.

After signing the General Act, Sweden-Norway duly ratified the convention on 24 April the same year. A protocol was signed on 19 April 1886 formally recognising that Sweden had deposited the ratification instruments in the archives of the German government.[45]

Congo Convention

As mentioned, even before the General Act was signed in Berlin, most countries at the conference were lining up to sign bilateral agreements with the International Congo Association, which was obviously going to be accepted as the main custodian and administrator of the "Congo Free State." On 10 February 1885, a bilateral convention was signed by Bildt and Strauch, on behalf of King Oscar and King Leopold (as founder of the association).[46]

The first four articles concern foreign relations and free trade. Sweden-Norway recognised the association as a friendly state. For its part, the association agreed to refrain from levying import taxes or licence duties etc. on Swedish and Norwegian subjects. The principle of most favoured nation was enshrined in the convention, so that should the association extend more favourable terms to a third party, those would automatically also apply to Sweden-Norway. Several articles (Arts. 5–10) regulated legal protection and judicial powers in quite an interesting way. The association undertook to protect the security and property of Swedish and Norwegian subjects, as well as assist in settling debts on behalf of Swedish-Norwegian traders. However, Sweden-Norway was allowed to appoint consuls in the Congo with judicial powers over Swedish and Norwegian subjects. To these subjects, Swedish and Norwegian law would apply. Although foreign subjects also had to follow laws enacted by the association, a Swede or Norwegian in breach of these laws was to be tried by the Swedish-Norwegian "tribunal consulaire." However, similar systems of consular jurisdiction were not uncommon in other parts of the world, and applied, for example, to Swedish subjects in China around this time (Cassel 2010). The slavery issue was also mentioned in a brief passage. In article 11, the Congo Association declares that it "will do all within its power" to fight slavery and the slave trade.[47]

---

45 Sveriges och Norges Traktater, Fjerde delen 1878-1885. Norstedts och söner, Stockholm, 1905.

46 The convention text can be found in Sandgren, C, Sverges Traktater, trettonde delen 1878-1890, Norstedts & söner Stockholm, 1905.

47 The entire Article 11 reads: « L'Association s'engage à faire tout ce qui est en son pouvoir pour empêcher la traite et supprimer l'esclavage. »

The ratification of the convention with the International Congo Association took place in Stockholm on 24 April and in Brussels on 11 June 1885, when ratification documents were also exchanged.[48]

---

48. Sverges Traktater, trettonde delen 1878-1890, Norstedts & söner Stockholm, 1905.

Discussion: What was Sweden doing in Berlin?

From the foregoing account, we now know that the Swedish government took a keen interest in the Berlin conference, and although Sweden-Norway was not within the inner circle of interested parties, the kingdoms were party to the Berlin General Act and signed a bilateral cooperation agreement with Leopold's Congo Association. We also know something of what Sweden-Norway did in Berlin and how it positioned itself. What, however, made the Swedish government so interested in the negotiations in Berlin, concerning a part of the world over which it had no direct claim? The king's envoy was preoccupied with the conference for four months. The king himself, the foreign ministry as well as Swedish legations from Washington in the west to Yokohama in the east busied themselves following the outcome of the negotiations.

From other accounts, we also know that hundreds of Swedes, Norwegians and Danes later participated in the exploitation and brutal colonisation of the people and resources of the Congo.

What drove these people to leave Scandinavia for the Congo? Were the Swedish military men, sea captains and missionaries in the Congo linked with the political activities in Berlin 1884-85? In general, how did Sweden-Norway fit into the age of New Imperialism around the turn of the last century?

The role of the historian is not just to "tell it the way it really was." While historical accounts must build on an empirical basis and "objective" data, this data must always be interpreted and understood in its context. The historian has to make these interpretations in an attempt to understand and explain why things happen. He or she should also try to understand why some things do not happen, or why certain events are forgotten. In the words of Eric Hobsbawm (1997), the role of the historian is to examine critically and reassess those parts of our collective past excluded from mainstream accounts. Sometimes these aspects of our history do not fit with the image that we – as a state or collective identity – construct to describe or legitimise our present state of affairs as well as our desired futures. What has been presented in this paper is arguably incongruent with the common perception that Sweden lacks a colonial history. Sweden did not acquire territories in Africa after the Berlin conference, but through the Berlin and Brussels agreements of 1885, King Oscar II and Baron Gillis Bildt enabled Sweden-Norway to get "a piece of the African cake" (as King Leopold once put it) even without *de facto* colonisation.

I now discuss the different plausible interests of the Swedish government and its key agents at the Berlin conference, grouped around four categories of motive: political, economic, ideological and personal. These categories do not derive from a specific theoretical or preconceived structure, but from my own reading of archival sources. The four groups of motives are comprehensive but not exhaustive. I reiterate that my research findings are preliminary, with much empirical data yet to be retrieved and studied. Of necessity, what follows is partly speculative. Nevertheless, it may contribute to a more nuanced and balanced picture of Sweden-Norway's foreign policies towards Africa during the age of New Imperialism. This will hopefully be a first step in piecing together a more complex yet coherent narrative of Sweden's historic relationship with remote and resource-rich areas, involving many, sometimes conflicting motives and interests.

Political motives

It is not obvious that there was much domestic political advantage for the Swedish king and his officials in the Berlin Conference or any potentially costly African colonial adventure. However, the political utility of the Swedish-Norwegian presence and agency in Berlin from a foreign relations perspective is much more easily understood. In Oscar's larger project of building closer political ties with Germany, the West Africa conference could have been a useful bargaining chip, or token of Sweden-Norway's allegiance. Bildt – who as royal envoy had a general instruction to strengthen links with the German Empire – explicitly proposed a general Swedish alignment with Germany's position during the conference.[49] When Bildt for once conveyed a suggestion from the Swedish government during the negotiations – relating to slavery and the slave trade – it was mainly the German reaction that was conveyed back to Stockholm.

Furthermore, King Oscar was known to have a keen interest in international politics. One can understand that the invitation to participate in a high-level conference involving all the major powers would have seemed like an excellent opportunity to play along in the game of world politics and to gain important information. Moreover, for a small country like Sweden-Norway, being seen alongside superpowers such as Britain, Germany, the US and Russia lent a certain prestige and importance. However, some contemporary observers were not so easily impressed. In the words of the American political scientist and socialist leader Daniel de Leon in 1886, the political landscape at the conference was a matter of the "giant" Bismarck being surrounded by "pygmies." He continued that, while the representatives of various countries, including Sweden-Norway, "strutted over the stage, believing they had in hand weighty questions of international law and were originating principles of far-reaching importance, they were, in fact, one and all, either led or driven as Prince Bismarck pointed the way, for purposes with which they had no concern" (de Leon, 1886).

In Oscar's private letters to Bildt – whom the king trusted not only as a capable diplomat but also as a friend and close confidant – we get some insight into

---

49. Bildt to Hochschild, 27/10/1884. RA: UD1902, Vol 4617a.

how the Berlin conference was seen as an inroad into European "big politics." In a letter of 7 December 1884 – when negotiations on the main declaration text were drawing to a close – the king shared his private thoughts about the conference.

> I have followed with interest the so called Congo conference, but one question has above all occupied my mind: Is Germany's new and sometimes surprisingly active colonial policy the main objective, or is it really a means to lure its western neighbour even further down the same path, and thus over time weaken her and distract attention from Elsas Lothringen?[50]

This is one of the few sources in which we hear from Oscar himself his thoughts about the conference. The three volumes of Oscar's memoirs, published after his death by the royal court, are completely silent on the subject. However, in this letter he discusses he conference in terms of European power politics, specifically the balance between Germany, France and Britain as well as the omnipresent danger of radicalism and socialism. What Oscar seems to be particularly grappling with in this exchange with his friend in Berlin, is how to fit the conference – as well as his peers' urge for colonies – into his political and social map of Europe.

In his reply to Oscar, Bildt offers an analysis of how the conference was connected to European power politics. Bildt concludes that Germany, through its colonial ambitions, on one hand wants to neutralise the French desire for revenge for defeat in 1871 and on the other aggravate the tensions between France and Britain. But, he discloses, the prime objective of the conference seems to go beyond these objectives: it serves to promote German colonial expansion in order to improve export markets and to "nourish and maintain German civil pride." In Bildt's view, the Berlin Conference was indeed part of a bigger strategy orchestrated by Bismarck concerning economic development and nation-building.[51]

Hence, a plausible interpretation would be that if Sweden-Norway wanted to remain relevant to Europe's political life, there could be advantages to attending the conference. The "cost" of attending was minor, while staying away could prove very costly politically in the long run. The conference itself also provided a wealth of information on the European political landscape. If the conference could, in addition, be used as a platform to support Bismarck and strengthen the relationship with Germany without incurring costs or domestic sacrifices, so much the better!

---

50. Oscar to Bildt, 7/12/1884. RA: Gillis Bildts arkiv, Vol 1. A transcript of the letter (in Swedish) is attached in appendix 3.
51. Brevkoncept, Bildt to Oscar 17/12/1884. RA: Gillis Bildts arkiv, Vol 1.

Economic motives

From what is known today, there were no major Swedish investments or commercial interests in the Congo at the time of the conference. Sweden had entertained colonial ambitions in the West Indies and in the Far East for most of the 18th century, during which time it also acquired the Saint-Barthélemy slave station (Muller 2004). The idea of establishing colonies outside Europe resurfaced in the 1840s as a solution to the shortage of agricultural land in the face of population growth (Stråth 2012:302). All these ambitions came to naught and after 1878, when Saint-Barthelémy was disposed of, Sweden no longer had colonies in the South. During the 18th century, trade in goods from the South formed a substantial part of Sweden's economy. Colonial commodities (kolonialvaror) such as tea, coffee, sugar and pigments were imported by the Swedish East India Company. While most of the tea was re-exported, the other commodities amounted to as much as 17 per cent of the total value of Swedish imports in 1770 (Muller 2004). As Rönnbäck (2009) argues, for much of the 1800s the Baltic economies were well integrated into the North-Atlantic slave-based economic system, where cotton and sugar were exchanged for exports of, for example, iron. But were there any economic prospects for Sweden and Norway in a European colonial expansion in Africa?

In the last decades of the 19th century, 80 per cent of Sweden's trade was with Britain, Germany and the other Nordic countries (Johansson and Norman 1986). Trade with Africa was minor, although some critical imports came from Africa, notably guano for agriculture (Stråth 2012:313). The placement of Sweden-Norway's consulates gives a good indication of where Sweden's primary trade interests lay. As Emanuelson (1980) notes, Sweden-Norway had 31 consulates in 1885. Of these, six were in Germany, two in France, three in the Mediterranean region, while no fewer than eight consulates were in Latin America. The remaining 12 were dispersed around the world, with only one in Africa in 1904, in Cape Town, far removed from the Congo. Still, Africa and particularly South Africa were not of negligible interest to Swedish traders and shipping companies in the 1880s. In that decade, some 60 to 80 Swedish freight ships per year hauled goods to and from South African harbours (Nygaard 2009). It is important to note that Norway and Sweden combined had one of the largest merchant fleets in the world at the end of the 19th century. In 1890, their total shipping tonnage grossed over 2 million, surpassed only by Britain (Larsson 2000:23). Clearly, any international agreement that could affect the fortunes of Sweden-Norway's shipping industry could not be ignored by the foreign ministry.

In December 1884, as Bildt prepared a bilateral agreement with Leopold's International Association, he wrote to his minister in Stockholm justifying the agreement on the grounds that "our fellow countrymen in one way or the other, have or will have, interests to protect in the Congo."⁵² However, a few weeks earlier he had confessed in a private letter to King Oscar that "our interests there are negligible."⁵³ If indeed Swedish-Norwegian interests in the Congo were negligible in 1884, in economic terms they did not increase in the 15 years following the conference. According to a report submitted to the ministry for foreign affairs in January 1903, the value of imports from Sweden and Norway to the Congo in the years 1899-1902 never exceeded 0.1 per cent of the total value of all imports.⁵⁴

It is thus difficult to argue that direct and short-term economic benefits were an important driving force for Sweden-Norway at the Berlin Conference. There may, however, have been high hopes on the Swedish side for a lucrative future business with the Congo and this may have been a contributing factor, especially given that the conference secured Swedish-Norwegian access to trade and enterprise in the Congo at negligible cost.

Economic motives could, also, have been a driving force in a more indirect way. Playing the Berlin game cleverly would allow Bildt to further reinforce the friendship with Germany, one of Sweden's most important trading partners. In the long term, substantial economic benefits could be expected for Swedish business from intensified trade with Germany, especially in iron and steel. It was of great interest for Sweden-Norway to be granted terms of trade on a "most favoured nation" basis with a unified Germany after 1871. In this context, it is worth noting that the German *Reichstag* officially granted Sweden-Norway such status on 20 February 1885 (Werner 1989:37), only six days before the official signing of the General Act in Berlin. Perhaps one should not interpret the German decision as a direct reward to Oscar for supporting Germany at the conference. However, it would be surprising if this bilateral consideration was not factored in by Bildt and Hochschild in formulating Swedish strategy and in taking a consistently pro-German position in Berlin.

Ideological motives

Ideas are important in politics. Demker (2007) even argues that ideas and principles can be more important than economic motives in foreign policy. I have already shown that the Swedish minister for foreign affairs explained in plain French that Sweden-Norway had no ambitions to establish colonies in Africa, but that he considered it a moral obligation to participate in the "noble mission" to spread Christianity and civilisation in Africa. Hochschild argued that without this "higher cause," Sweden-Norway could just as well have stayed away

---

52. Bildt to Hochschild, "enskildt," 27/12/1884.RA: UD1902, Vol 4617a.
53. "våra intressen der är äro obetydliga." Brevkoncept, Bildt till Oscar 5/12/1884. RA: Gillis Bildts arkiv, Vol 1.
54. Skandinaver i Kongostaten. RA: UD 1902, Vol 4619.

from the conference. He prompted Bildt to engage in the negotiations on slavery, clearly also on ideological grounds. Based on what King Oscar wrote to his "brother" Leopold in Belgium, we can assume that he too, at least nominally, shared Hochschild's position: it was a moral obligation to contribute to Leopold's civilising mission in Africa and thus work for the best interests of humankind. In addition, Oscar thought that by supporting Bismarck, he would lend a hand in the fight against socialism, republicanism and other "vices."

How well did this view chime with that of the government and, indeed, the Swedish political elite? Ideas about the moral responsibility of Western civilisation – Scandinavian and Germanic cultures in particular – to fight "barbarism" had a strong foothold among large groups of the Swedish cultural and political establishment of the period. Throughout much of the 19th century, ideas were reproduced about the cultural as well as political "historical mission" of the Scandinavian people (Elvander 1961). This cultural nationalism of the first part of the century was clearly associated with *Skandinavism*, but there was also a sense of duty to promote humankind as well. For example, an influential daily newspaper argued in 1854 that the objective of the Scandinavian people was "to again become a sovereign power, able to stand up against Russian savagery and clear the way for freedom and civilisation among the oppressed tribes of Russia."[55]

From the 1880s, Swedish nationalism became more conservative, and much of the ideological public debate took on more social-Darwinistic elements. While the early cultural nationalism contained a moral obligation to promote civilisation, gradually this "mission" was mixed with ideas about the need to join a larger pan-Germanic struggle to fight other races, considered to be of lower standing (Elvander 1961). Thus, the idea of a duty to participate in a noble mission to civilise Africa, expressed both by the Swedish foreign minister and the king, fits into a longer ideological trend in which racial biology and social Darwinism gained a certain acceptance in political and scientific life in Sweden. This trend – in which discrimination against Swedish ethnic minorities, for example, the *Sapmi* people, and the "colonisation" of Northern Sweden should also be placed – extended well into the 1930s (Stråth 2012:459ff). Obviously, Sweden was no stranger to Eurocentric cultural civilisation, which implied taking up "The White Man's Burden," as Rudyard Kipling put it in 1899. These ideals of promoting "Christianity and Civilisation" can clearly be traced in Swedish newspaper reporting of the Berlin Conference of 1884–85.[56]

One cannot discuss ideological motives without mentioning the substantial missionary activities pursued by Swedish Christian organisations. In Europe in

---

55. Translated quote from Göteborgs Handels- och Sjöfartstidning 19-21 July 1854, in Elvander (1961).
56. See Carl Yngfalk's study.

the 1870s, there was a growing public interest in Africa. Commercial interests mingled with *noblesse oblige*, a sense of duty to civilise Africa. This widespread European cultural phenomenon gained a strong foothold in Scandinavia especially from the 1870s through the evangelical movements. About 100 Swedish missionaries arrived in the Congo between 1878 and 1903. In his seminal work, Sigbert Axelsson (1970) describes the Swedish mission in Congo with refreshing honesty. He attributes, at least in part, the relatively large mission in the Congo to the public impact of Stanley's expeditions in search of David Livingstone. Axelsson's study offers interesting insights into how Swedes viewed the nature of their "civilising mission" and how they regarded the "objects" of civilisation.

Obviously, some of the Swedish army officers working in the Congo did not think highly of the Congolese people. Lieutenant Peter August Möller in 1887 depicted the Congolese as "mendacious and cowardly, indolent and vain, and deceitful and ungrateful." This people, of a "half-human nature" are characterised by "want of development" and they "lack depth and could never resolve themselves for any kind of bold action or decisive steps." Another Swedish officer, Lieutenant Wester, claimed in 1886 that "the inhabitants of Central Africa, who live in a luxuriant land, are particularly inclined to indolence, [and therefore] the work of civilising must be aimed at teaching them to understand the necessity of work" (Axelsson 1970:223ff). Teaching the local people to work in the context of Leopold's Congo Association typically meant forced labour and gruesome punishment for those who refused, as Adam Hochschild describes in his bestselling book of 1998.

Did Swedish missionaries share these views of the Congolese, and what was the role of the Swedish Christian missions in the Congo terror regime? While many missionaries voiced their frustrations at local people's "indolence and laziness," most missionaries at least emphasised the good intellectual capacity of the Congolese people (Axelsson 1970:226). In terms of the relationship between Europeans and Congolese, however, the missionaries were not very different from other whites. Axelsson concedes that the entire colonial enterprise, missions included, was built on a master-servant system, including slavery. While the "colonial enterprise" aimed – among other things – to combat the slave trade, the missionaries were no strangers to the practice of buying children to keep at mission stations. In the missionaries' view, this was in the children's spiritual and physical best interests. The missionary C.J. Engvall, in a letter dated 1881, reported that he had eight children: "… the majority of them we have bought from the king, so that they are the exclusive property of the mission …" Each child cost between six and seven pounds (Axelsson 1970:245). This account sheds interesting light on the discussion four years later in Berlin about whether equal efforts should be made to eradicate the slave trade and slavery. In Berlin, it was argued that slavery was too deeply embedded in African social life and that the slave trade should be tackled first. Ironically, Christian missionaries from Sweden – part of the ideological *avant garde* of Europe's civilising project in Africa – themselves considered buying children a useful method for their cause, and kept them as "property" at the stations.

An even more critical view of Swedish missionaries in the Congo in the decades around 1900 was taken by Raoul J. Granqvist (2008), who argues that the missionaries were simply part and parcel of the colonial regime. While the missionaries did not themselves seek to exploit the resources of the Congo or the people's labour, there were strong ties between the military and religious wings of the colonial project. Whenever the missions had security problems, needed protection of property or simply were annoyed with the cultural habits and expressions of local people, they would rely on the brute force of the International Congo Association, its judges and military strength to help them out. Colonialism – says Granqvist – was no less brutal and reckless when performed by Swedish missionaries. He also connects the Swedish mission's operations in the Congo with the wider ideological movements during the 1800s outlined above that Western civilisation had a duty to civilise "people of lower standing" whether in the Congo, Russia or Northern Sweden.

In sum, it is relatively straightforward to discern a strand of ideology among Swedes participating in the Congo colonisation project. In addition, ideology should not be dismissed from Sweden-Norway's actions at the Berlin Conference. The duty for Christian civilisations to civilise "lower races" was prominent in political life in Sweden throughout the most of the 1800s. These ideas were explicitly referred to by the minister for foreign affairs as well as King Oscar in official communications. The sources studied do not allow us to ascertain how genuine these ideological expressions were. Were the minister and king "true believers" willing to shoulder the "White Man's Burden," or were they just paying lip service while harbouring ulterior motives? In any event, ideology is not irrelevant to explaining Sweden-Norway's actions in Berlin, even if only as a rhetorical or cultural tool of legitimation.

Personal motives

Finally, could there have been personal motives at play among the main Swedish actors at the Berlin Conference? Of course, in the case of Oscar II, there is little if any distinction between the man and the monarch. Whatever affected the kingdoms and monarchy also affected Oscar as a person, and in his case it will always be difficult to separate personal from political or economic motives. We have also seen that Oscar took a keen interest in closer relations with Germany, which he saw as a protector of the *ancièn régime* in Europe against democratic reforms and "radicalism." While he defended monarchy as an institution, he also fought for his own position as well as that of his descendants. The Berlin

Conference furthermore offered a possibility to engage – if only marginally – in one of his personal interests, the big politics of Europe. One may speculate that after the humiliating constitutional defeat in Norway during the spring of 1884 regarding the monarchy's powers, the invitation to the Berlin Conference was a source of consolation and respite for the king. Moreover, here was a chance to interact as a peer with the great Bismarck, whom he admired.

We know that Gillis Bildt at least found his assignment rewarding at a more personal level. In a draft of a letter to King Oscar, Bildt expresses his gratitude at have being entrusted with representing the king at the conference. In Bildt's words, for him it was "interesting and instructive to take part of such a large conference."[57] Upon his appointment as envoy in Berlin in 1874, Bildt had doubted his qualifications and limited language capabilities (SBL). Ten years later, Bildt was still eager to learn and expand his experience as diplomat and statesman, and the Berlin Conference would have provided an excellent opportunity.

What Foreign Minister Hochschild personally thought about the Berlin Conference or African colonisation we cannot tell from the sources studied to date. Hochschild, described by a British diplomat as "the Frenchman of the Nordic countries," would resign his post in 1885 after pushing for a more liberal constitutional reform of the union. While he was an old school aristocrat, he is said to have often embraced liberal ideas (SBL). In the case of the Berlin Conference, Hochschild notably stressed the anti-slavery issue. Hence, if there was a personal motive on his part, it transcends the ideological motives discussed previously: it would have been a personal mission to press for liberal ideas against slavery and to promote Christianity and civilisation.

Personal motives are "slippery" in the sense that they merge with other motives and often leave no clear traces in the sources, so one should be careful not to give them too much weight. Nevertheless, human history does play out through the agency of people and personal motives cannot be ignored. In particular, at distinct events like the Berlin Conference, they may be significant.

---

57. "Konferensen går bra, ty det ser ut som om den skulle komma till att [entrainer] resultat, men fort går det ej, och ibland litet konfyst. Jag är mycket tacksam för det n. förtroendet att äfven der få representera E.Mt., ty om ock våra intressen der är äro obetydliga så äro dock [arbetet der intressant]… [och lärorikt …att …vara med på ett hörn uti en så stor konferens]." Bildt's draft is edited several times and its exact final wording is not possible to gauge from the draft. It provides important insight into personal motives and emotions. Bildt to Oscar, concept, 5/12/1884. RA: Gillis Bildts arkiv, Vol 1.

Conclusions: a "new" colonial past for Sweden?

In coming years, it is likely that more information will become available that will deepen and enrich the picture of Swedish colonial history. More sources need to be examined, and not only official government records. What did leaders of Swedish trade and industry think and do in relation to Africa in the period? How did Africa as a potential market or resource base fit into the landscape of Sweden's industrialisation? How were the Berlin Conference and Scramble discussed and reflected in media and public discourse? How did the other envoys at the Berlin Conference regard Sweden-Norway?

Naturally, more and more questions surface. It would surely be of great interest to study in more detail what the Swedish actors did in the period after the conference. Once the political rules of engagement had been settled, were there serious attempts by Swedish or Norwegian entrepreneurs, traders and businessmen to exploit the potential benefits of the Congo? If not, why? And how did the Swedish government react as international criticism of Leopold's reign of terror in the Congo grew in the early 1900s?

While follow-up questions abound, it is nevertheless possible to tease out some conclusions from what has been presented so far. It is beyond doubt that Sweden-Norway took an active part in the Berlin Conference, fully supporting, signing and ratifying the resultant General Act. The Berlin Conference directly involved the very highest stratum of the government, namely King Oscar, Minister for Foreign Affairs Count Hochschild, and the Swedish envoy in Berlin, Gillis Bildt. It is also obvious that Sweden-Norway was not one of the key players and did not take regular part in the detailed negotiations. When the conference started, the Swedish government did not to have a premeditated strategy or precise position. In the course of the conference, some Swedish positions were worked out in Stockholm, based on which the Swedish envoy did try to influence the conference outcome. To summarise what we know about the Swedish-Norwegian position or strategy, it aimed to secure terms of trade as most favoured nation; to underscore the civilising mission of colonisation in Africa; and to generally rally behind Germany in the negotiations.

By ratifying the General Act, Sweden-Norway condoned the colonial exploitation of Africa by European powers on the terms laid down by the Berlin Conference, even if this exploitation was clothed as a "noble mission of civilisation." The conference gave Sweden-Norway the same privileges as the other signatories with respect to the trade on the Congo and Niger. In order for Swedish and Norwegian businessmen to fully exploit the terms offered by the conference, the government of Sweden-Norway rapidly signed a bilateral agreement with King Leopold's International Congo Association. We also know that many Swedish soldiers, sea captains and missionaries took an active part in the colonisation of the Congo precipitated by the conference.

Determining the actual motives behind Swedish involvement in Berlin and in the Congo is a difficult task. At this stage, I have only offered a set of possible explanations. It seems no one single cause or driving force explains Sweden-Norway's activities in Berlin or in the Scramble. Of the possible motives discussed, a combination of indirect or long-term economic benefits arising from trade and ideological drivers seem to have been prominent. Possibly, a Scandinavian version of the motto "Commerce, Christianity and Civilisation" may have been sufficient to justify Sweden-Norway's involvement, especially as there were really no costs involved at this stage.

A parallel to the logic of Sweden-Norway's involvement could also be found in the discussion of what drove the Scramble for Africa at large. Chamberlain (2010:80ff) hypothesises that the "hasty grab" of the 1880s was merely a way of staking claims for the future. While there was no real economic or political sense to the rapid annexation of territories in Africa at the time, it was more a matter of protecting one's spheres of influence. The hasty grab was thus to ensure that no other power would step in and seize control of the trade, the resource base or potential markets. This is also consistent with the *Torschlusspanik* experienced in Germany just before the Berlin Conference (Pakenham 2002:205). All the other powers were pegging claims in Africa and, simply put, there was a fear of being left behind. To what extent was the logic of the "hasty grab" or the *Torschlusspanik* applicable to Sweden-Norway as well?

It is safe to say that Sweden-Norway had relatively small economic interests in the region. On the other hand, shipping was an important business activity, especially in the Norwegian economy (Emanuelsson 1980:145; Larsson 2000). Therefore it was in principle of interest to Sweden-Norway that the Congo and Niger Rivers be kept under a free trade regime. Furthermore, the same urgency embedded in the *Torschlusspanik* can be discerned in Sweden-Norway's actions to secure a trade agreement with the International Congo Association. As Bildt commented, it would not be pleasant to be "last on the list."

Sweden-Norway never acquired colonies in Africa in the Scramble. Neither did the state invest heavily in enterprises on the continent. But is it possible to maintain that Sweden lacks a colonial history in Africa? If the answer is no, what difference does it make? As indicated earlier, virtually all historical accounts of Sweden and Swedish foreign policy in the 19th century are silent on the Berlin Conference. One may argue that it was a peripheral event for Sweden, not meriting a place in history books. But even when the Conference is mentioned – as in Stråth (2012) – Sweden's role is omitted. The Berlin Conference has been also been left out of biographies. This applies to King Oscar's three volume memoirs, but also to the main biography of Swedish celebrities and officials, *Svenskt*

Biografiskt Lexikon. The *Lexikon* often contains detailed biographies. The article on Bildt describes his time as envoy in Berlin, but does not contain a word on the West Africa conference. Perhaps Sweden is not free of colonial history, but mainstream literature is certainly free of colonial history writing.

How does a Swedish colonial past relate to narratives that construct and shape Swedish identity? As Maria Eriksson Baaz argues (2002), the construction of the identity of a developed and enlightened "self" as contrasted with the indolent and underdeveloped "other" among modern Swedish development aid workers in Tanzania takes its vocabulary and structural patterns straight out of the colonial library. Interestingly, there appears be a line connecting the present ethical order and self-image of Swedes to the "White Man's Burden" discourse of the Scramble. However, Sweden-Norway's role at the Berlin Conference or in the larger story of colonisation and European world domination has not figured in the narratives around which collective national identity has been built. Until now, I would argue, it is rather "the lack of colonial past" that has shaped our collective identity in relation to Africa.

The Swedish self-image and identity in global politics and development has since the Cold War era been closely associated with the imagery of a small non-partisan country without the moral burden of a colonial past. As argued by political scientist Ulf Bjereld (2007), during the Cold War, Swedish governments were anxious to show the world that Sweden's neutrality rested primarily on a moral foundation. The legitimacy of Sweden's staying out of East-West military dualism was seen to be strengthened by an active policy towards the South, based on moral grounds and principles of solidarity. This gave rise to the creation of a relatively large organisation for development assistance, and high government spending on aid from the 1960s onwards. Development assistance thus became an operational instrument for realisation of the vision for the future– a world free of poverty.

If Sweden's foreign policy was to be on a moral foundation, the image – constructed or not – of Sweden as a nation without a colonial past was of course an asset: the lack of colonial past legitimised Sweden's agency in Africa. The Swedish government has also used this asset repeatedly in its formulation of foreign policy vis-à-vis Africa. In 2008, the Swedish government developed a new strategy for relations with Africa, where it was stated that "Sweden's lack of a colonial past in Africa and the fact that the north European social model has served as an inspiration for many African countries mean that Sweden is well placed to influence, cooperate and act."[58] Eleven years earlier, a similar

---

58. Sveriges Regering, "Sweden and Africa — a policy to address common challenges and opportunities", Government Communication 2007/08:67, 2008, p. 21.

narrative about "lack of colonial past in Africa" was used in connection with the previous strategy.[59]

Indeed, the principle of solidarity in combination with the "lack of colonial past" have been central elements in government development cooperation policy for the last 50 years (Wohlgemuth 2012; Odén and Wohlgemuth, undated). In line with this perspective, Odén and Stålgren (2007) write that Sweden "in all important aspects" lacked a colonial past, which led to a high "demand" for aid from the supposedly disinterested, small and neutral country. By contrast, Öhman (2007) in a study of Swedish development assistance in Tanzania in the 1960s and 1970s, argues that such assistance was never disinterested. In Öhman's account, development assistance was used as one way to catch up with other European powers in Africa, which had gained a headstart in new markets through their earlier colonial enterprises. Regardless of which of these interpretations one prefers, clearly the historical narrative of Sweden's colonial innocence has been matched with a vision for the future of Africa in which Swedish development assistance and other bilateral cooperation had a prominent role.

Recent decades have seen Swedish foreign policy in the South move away from the moral imperative and focus more on mutual interests. Ten years ago, the Swedish parliament laid down the Policy on Global Development whereby development assistance was to be seen as one of many ways of promoting global development.[60] The focus has slowly been shifting from solidarity to global public goods and "enlightened self-interest" (Odén and Stålgren 2007). In a way, this also creates a wider frame for discussing Sweden's role in global development in a longer context.

In sum, there is more to find out about Sweden's colonial history. As these stories unfold, we should be prepared to reassess Sweden's image and identity in the global South. We should encourage a discourse on what principles, ideas and driving forces have shaped – and continue to shape – Swedish actors' involvement in global processes regarding material structures, resources, development as well as power formations. Not least, who has the power to construct and reconstruct the collective identities, self-images and world-views that we carry with us and that ultimately shape human interaction on this planet. Whether the production of a more complete and "true" history of Sweden's colonial history will enable a new Swedish identity to emerge, and a new vision of African futures to be shaped, remains to be seen. One thing is sure: historians can contribute to this discourse.

---

59. Sveriges Regering, "Partner med Afrika. Förslag till en ny svensk politik för våra kontakter med Afrika söder om Sahara", Utrikesdepartementet, 1997.
60. Regeringens Proposition 2002/03:122, Gemensamt ansvar: Sveriges politik för global utveckling, 2003.

LITERATURE

Angell, Svein Ivar. "Konsulatspörsmålet og kolonialismen," in Kjerland and Rio (eds), *Kolonitid: nordmenn på eventyr og big business i Afrika og Stillehavet*, Oslo: Scandinavian Academic Press, 2009, pp. 111–27.

Avango, Dag. Sveagruvan: s*vensk gruvhantering mellan industri, diplomati och geovetenskap 1910–1934*, Stockholm: Jernkontoret, 2005.

Avango, Dag, Annika E Nilsson and Peder Roberts. "Assessing Arctic futures: Voices, resources and governance". *Polar Journal,* DOI:10.1080/2154896X.2013.790197, June 2013.

Axelson, Sigbert. *Culture confrontation in the lower Congo*. Doctoral dissertation, Uppsala Univ. Falköping:Gummesson, 1970.

Baaz, Maria Eriksson. *The white wo/man's burden in the age of partnership. A postcolonial reading of identity in development aid*. Dissertation, Dept. of Peace and Development Research. Gothenburg University, 2002.

Bjereld, Ulf. "Svensk utrikespolitik i ett historiskt perspektiv," in Brommesson and Ekengren (eds), *Sverige i Världen*. Malmö: Gleerups, 2007.

Cassel, Pär. "Traktaten som aldrig var och fördraget som nästan inte blev. De svensk–norsk–kinesiska förbindelserna 1847–1909", *Historisk Tidsskrift*, 130:3 (2010): 437–66.

Chamberlain, M.E. *The scramble for Africa*. Harlow: Pearson Educational, 3rd ed., 2010.

Demker, Marie. "Idéer, normer, identiteter och diskurser i utrikespolitiken," in Brommesson, D. and A-M Ekengren s), *Sverige i Världen*. Malmö: Gleerups, 2007.

Elvander, Nils. "Från liberal skandinavism till konservativ nationalism i Sverige", föredrag vid nordiska historikermötet i Lund 1961, reprinted in Scandia 2008.

Emanuelsson, Kjell. *Den svensk-norska utrikesförvaltningen 1870–1905. Dess organisations-och verksamhetsförändring*. Lund: CWK Gleerup, 1980.

Gunnarsson, Christer and Mauricio Rojas. *Tillväxt, stagnation, kaos. En institutionell studie av underutvecklingens orsaker och utvecklingens möjligheter*. SNS Förlag, 1995.

Granqvist, Raoul J. "Med Gud och kung Leopold i ryggen: en berättelse om svensk mission i Kongo", Ord & Bild, 2 (2008): 98–117.

Griffiths, Ieuan. "The Scramble for Africa: Inherited Political Boundaries." *Geographical Journal*, 152, 2 (1986):204–16

Hochschild, A. *King Leopold's ghost: A story of greed, terror, and heroism in Colonial Africa*. Boston: Houghton Mifflin, 1998.

Johansson, Alf and Torbjörn Norman. "Den svenska neutralitetspolitiken i ett historiskt perspektiv," in Hugemark, B. (ed.), *Neutralitet och försvar. Perspektiv på svensk säkerhetspolitik 1809–1985*, Stockholm: Militärhistoriska förlaget, 1986.

Kjerland, Kirsten Alsaker and Knut Mikjel Rio (eds), *Kolonitid: nordmenn på eventyr og big business i Afrika og Stillehavet*. Oslo: Scandinavian Academic, 2009.

Larsson, Berit. *Svenska varor på svenska kölar. Staten, industrialiseringen och linjesjöfartens framväxt i Sverige 1890–1925*, Meddelanden från Ekonomisk-Historiska Institutionen, Göteborgs Universitet, 2000.

de Leon, Daniel. "The Conference at Berlin on the West-African Question." *Political Science Quarterly*, 1, 1 (Mar. 1886):103–39.

Lindberg, Folke. *Den svenska utrikes politikens historia III:4, 1872–1914*. Stockholm: Norstedts, 1958.

Linde, Rolf. "Gillis Bildt – ett arkiv som vittnar om förtroende", EB-nytt, 2004, Riksarkivet. pp. 16–19.

Lindqvist, Herman. *Historien om Sverige. Ånga och dynamit,* Stockholm: Norstedts, 1999.

Miller, Charles. *The Lunatic Express*, First published Macmillan, 1971, London: Penguin, 2001.

Muller, Leos. "Kolonialprodukter i Sveriges handel och konsumtionskultur, 1700–1800", *Historisk Tidsskrift*, 124, 2 (2004):225–48.

Nationalencyklopedin, Höganäs: Bra Böcker, 1990. Articles: "Bildt, Gillis" and "Berlinkonferensen"

Nationalencyklopedin, Malmö: Nationalencyklopedin AB, 2009. Article: "Berlinkonferensen".

Nygaard, Knut M. "Norsk seilskipsfart på Sör-Afrika", in Kjerland and Rio (2009).

Odén, Bertil and Patrik Stålgren. "Sverige och internationellt utvecklingssamarbete", in Brommesson and Ekengren, 2007.

Odén, Bertil and Lennart Wohlgemuth. "Svensk biståndspolitik i ett internationellt perspektiv", Perspectives No.1, Gothenburg University, undated.

Olofsson, Rune Pär. *En kung i varje tum. Roman om Oscar II*. Höganäs: Bra bok, 1985.

Oscar II. *Mina memoarer* , vol 1–3. Sthlm: Norstedts, 1960–62.

Pakenham, Thomas. *The scramble for Africa,* first published 1991, London: Abacus, 2002 (paperback edition).

Reeves, Jesse S. "The Origin of the Congo Free State, Considered from the Standpoint of International Law", *American Journal of International Law*, 3, 1 (Jan. 1909):99–118.

Rodney, Walter. *How Europe underdeveloped Africa,* Washington: Howard Univ. Press, 1972.

Rönnbäck, Klas. *Commerce and Colonisation. Studies of Early Modern Merchant Capitalism in the Atlantic Economy*, Doctoral Dissertation, University of Gothenburg, 2009.

SBL Svenskt Biografiskt Lexikon, online version, "Carl F L Hochschild", urn:sbl:13676, (art av Torsten Petré), accessed 2013-04-23.

SBL Svenskt biografiskt lexikon, online-version, "D A Gillis Bildt", urn:sbl:18208, (art av O. Hallendorff.), accessed 2013-04-23.

SBL Svenskt biografiskt lexikon, online-version, "Oscar II", urn:sbl:7812, (art av Torgny Nevéus), accessed 2013-04-23.

Southall, Roger. "Scrambling for Africa? Continuities and Discontinuities with Formal Imperialism," in Southall, Roger and Henning Melber (eds). *A new scramble for Africa? Imperialism, investment and development,* Scottsville: University of Kwa-Zulu Natal Press, 2009.

Southall, Roger and Henning Melber (eds). *A new scramble for Africa? Imperialism, investment and development,* Scottsville: University of Kwa-Zulu Natal Press, 2009.

Stråth, Bo. *Sveriges historia 1830–1920,* Stockholm: Norstedts, 2012.

Stråth, Bo. *Union och Demokrati: De förenade rikena Sverige-Norge 1814–1905,* Nora: Nya Doxa, 2005.

Tell, Per-Erik. *Detta fredliga uppdrag…om 522 svenskar i terrorns Kongo.* Umeå: h:ström Text och Kultur, 2005.

Werner, Yvonne Maria. *Svensk-tyska förbindelser kring sekelskiftet 1900. Politik och ekonomi vid tillkomsten av 1906 års svensk-tyska handels- och sjöfartstraktat.* Doctoral Dissertation. Lund: Lund University Press, 1989.

Wesseling, Henk. "The Netherlands and the Partition of Africa." *Journal of African History,* 22, 4 (1981):495–509.

Wesseling, Henk. *Söndra och härska: Uppdelningen av Afrika 1880–1914,* first published 1992, original title "Verdeel en heers. De deling van Afrika, 1880–1914", Swedish translation, Lund: Historiska media, 2006.

Wohlgemuth, Lennart. "Svenskt utvecklingssamarbete 50 år", Perspectives No. 23, University of Gothenburg, 2012.

Öhman, May-Britt. *Taming exotic beauties. Swedish hydropower construction in Tanzania in the era of development assistance, 1960s–1990s,* Doctoral Dissertation, Stockholm: KTH, 2007.

APPENDIX 1.

Transcript of document. RA: UD 1902 Vol 4617a. Hochschild till Bildt 26 Nov 1884

Copie d'une dépêche adressée par le Ministre des Affaires Etrangères au Ministre du Roi à Berlin en date Stockholm le 26 Novembre 1884.

En acceptant l'invitation collective des Gouvernements Allemand et Français de se faire représente dans la conférence de Berlin le gouvernement du Roi n'a eu an vue que de contribuer pour sa part à une œuvre essentiellement civilisatrice et à laquelle toutes les puissances chrétiennes ont par cela même un intérêt identique, indépendamment des avantages que leur commerce et leur navigation [peuvent] retirer du libre accès à des régions d'où elles avaient été exclues jusqu'à ce jour.

 Les Royaumes Unis n'ont plus de colonies et rien ne fait présager qu'ils cherchent dorénavant à en établir. Ils auraient pu rester étrangers à la conférence si son unique programme avait été l'établissement dans le bassin du Congo d'une autorité régulière capable d'y garantir la liberté du commerce et de la navigation, car l'esprit d'équité dont sont animés de nos jours les gouvernements européens en ce qui concerne ces importants intérêts leur assurait d'avance la participation aux bienfaits qui résulteront sans doute de l'entente des autres puissances. Mais le but de la conférence est plus élevé. Il s'agit de faire pénétrer le [christianité] et avec lui la civilisation dans des contrées livrées jusqu'à ce jour à la barbarie. Les pays scandinaves avaient l'obligation de prendre part à cette généreuse mission du moment que leur concours était demandé.

 Vous verrez par ce que je viens d'avoir l'honneur de vous dire quel est le role trâcé [rôle tracé] au représentant de la Suède et de la Norvège. Vous appuierez toutes les propositions tendant à la propagation de la civilisation chrétienne en Afrique ne sortant de la réserve, que les circonstances conseillent d'ailleurs, que si quelque décision de la conférence vous semblait dévier de la voie que le Gouvernement du Roi poursuit ou être de nature à retarder la réalisation de ce qui, à son point de vue, est le but essentiel de la conférence.

 Je crois utile à cet effet de vous signaler une expression du Projet de Déclaration soumis dès le principe à la conférence. Elle se trouve dans l'avant dernier paragraphe où it est dit que : « Toutes les puissances …. prendront l'obligation de concourir à la suppression de l'esclavage et surtout de la traite des noirs …. » Le mot « surtout» ainsi placé semble affaiblir l'engagement en ce qui concerne l'esclavage que cependant sans aucun doute toutes les puissances veulent concourir à supprimer avec la même ardeur et le même zèle que la traite.

 Je vous invite, Monsieur le Baron, à proposer la suppression de ce mot à moins que des raisons, justifiant selon vous son maintien ne vous soient donnés par vous collègues.

Agréez, etc..
Signé/Hochschild

APPENDIX 2.

Translation / Interpretation by David Nilsson of appendix 1:

Transcript of document. RA: UD1902 Vol 4617a. Hochschild till Bildt 26 Nov 1884.

Copy of a message sent from the Minister for Foreign Affairs to the Royal Minister in Berlin dated 26 November 1884, Stockholm

In accepting the joint invitation from the German and French governments to be represented at the Berlin conference, the Government of the King did not have in view anything other than to contribute for its part to an essentially civilising work, and for which all the Christian states share an identical interest, regardless of the benefits that their trade and navigation can secure through free access to areas from which they have previously been excluded.

The United Kingdoms [of Sweden and Norway] no longer have colonies and currently have no ambitions to establish such. [Sweden and Norway] could have remained indifferent to the conference if its only object was the establishment in the Congo Basin of an authority able to ensure freedom of trade and navigation, since the spirit of fairness that present European governments uphold concerning these important interests assures Sweden-Norway access to those benefits that, without doubt, result from other states' agreements. But the purpose of the conference is higher. It is to spread Christianity and with it civilisation in areas subjected so far to barbarism. Scandinavian countries have been obliged to take part in this noble mission from the moment their involvement was requested.

You will now see why I have just had the honour to give you this account of the trajectory of the role played by Sweden and Norway's representative. You shall support all proposals pertaining to the spreading of Christian civilisation in Africa without reservation, unless circumstances suggest otherwise, or if a decision of the conference appears to you to be a deviation from the government's intentions, or is of such a nature that it will hinder the accomplishment of what in the government's view is essentially the purpose of the conference.

I think it is useful to point out to you a passage in the Draft Declaration submitted at the beginning of the conference. It is to be found in the penultimate paragraph, where it is stated that: "All the powers ... have the obligation to work for the suppression of slavery and especially the slave trade ..." The word "especially" placed in such a manner, however, appears to weaken the commitment regarding slavery, which without doubt all the states wish to suppress with the same ardour and zeal as the slave trade.

I invite you, Baron, to propose the deletion of this word unless reasons which, in your view justify its being maintained, are given by your colleagues.

Accept, etc. ..
Signed / Hochschild

APPENDIX 3.

Transcript of letter from King Oscar to Gillis Bildt. In Gillis Bildts arkiv. Vol 1: Brevväxling kungliga personer.

Avskrift av brev – utdrag. Från Oscar II till Gillis Bildt. Stockholm, 7 Dec 1884.
(understrykningar i original)

Min käre vän. Jag har rätt länge tänkt skrifva till dig men alltid har något kommit emellan. Med intresse har jag följt den s.k. Congoconferencen, men <u>ett</u> har dervid framförallt sysselsatt mina tankar, neml den frågan. Är Tysklands nya och, i vissa fall, öfverraskande aktiva colonialpolitik hufvud-mål (ett mål kan den ju alltid sägas vara?) eller är den egentligen ett medel för att smickra in den vestra grannen <u>än längre</u> på samma väg, samt dermedelst på lång tid försvaga dels kraft och bortvända dels uppmärksamhet från Elsas Lothringen?

Jag kan nog inse att <u>deri</u> kan ligga en viss fördel för Tyska Riket, <u>om</u>, nemligen, det förmår bibehålla tyngden af militärbördan under <u>många</u> fredsår, men hvad jag likväl, under alla omständigheter, beklagar är att den nya förunderligt såta vänskapen med arvsfienden så tydligt göres gällande på alla punkter av verlden, i China som i Afrika, i Berlin som i Paris. Ty den stöder sakernas n.v. [nuvarande] ordning i Frankrike, och förlänger med en betänklig tid dess dåliga inflytande på alla monarkiska statsskick uti Europa. Tyskland får nog i sinom tid erfara detta, ty socialismen och radikalism äro infusioner mot hvilka hvarken [Strassburg och Metz?], eller värnpligt och strategie i längden hjälpa! Och det förekommer mig som i Tysklands inre politik redan nu en mera accentuerad opposition bedrifves mot Rikskanslerns politik, så att då hans förträffliga parlamentariska förmåga till och med är vanmäktig. Har jag rätt häri, eller ser jag ej djupt nog in i den tyska rikspolitiken? Är någon förbättring snart att emotse – ifall jag har lyckats ställningen för dagen rätt? Om dess ej ovigtiga frågor skulle jag önska få upplysningar av dig. Att Fursten hatar Gladstone vet jag och det förvånar mig i sanning ej. Men det kunde nog hända att G. för tillfället åtminstone reder sig ur klämman, särdeles ifall Gordon räddas hvilket ju ännu är en möjlighet. Och då blir den fientliga hållningen mot Gladstones person och ministére ju liktydigt med en fientlig politik emot England. ? Deri ser jag äfven en fara, och ett aflägsnande från den politiska framtid som förespeglat mig sedan så lång tid! Roligt om jag kunde få erfara dina tanka om allt detta.

….

[brevet fortsätter med andra ämnen, bl a frikännandet av August Strindberg, vilket upprör Oscar]

APPENDIX 4.

Transcript of letter from King Leopold II of Belgium, to Oscar II, dated 23/12/1884. RA: UD1902, Vol 4617b.

Sire, Votre Majesté, Protecteur éclairé des entreprises scientifiques et civilisatrices, a bien voulu a permettre de s'inscrire comme membre d'Honneur de l'œuvre que nous avons fondée pour pénétrer au cœur de l'Afrique et pour ouvrir cette contrée à toutes les nations.

Elle a daigné autoriser plusieurs brillants officiers de Sa belle armée à entrer au service de l'Association Internationale du Congo.

Des Stations importantes, chefs lieux de vastes districts au centre de l'Afrique, sont aujourd'hui dirigées par des Suédois.

Les Etats-Unis, l'Allemagne, l'Angleterre, l'Italie et l'Espagne ont reconnu le drapeau d'Association Internationale du Congo comme celui d'un Etat Ami et ont signé avec elle des conventions.

Je serais très hereux que Votre Majesté voulait bien charger son Gouvernement de traiter aussi avec l'Association. En m'accordant cette faveur, Elle me donnerait une nouvelle preuve de Ses sentiment á mon égard, dont je lui serait profondément reconnaissant.

Je me félicite de cette occasion qui m'est offerte de remercier Votre Majesté de Sa constante bienveillance pour moi et pour l'entreprise Africaine dont je m'occupe et je La prie de trouver ici l'expression de ma sincère inébranlable amitié.

C'est dans ces sentiments que je me dis toujours

Sire,
de Votre Majesté,
le bon Frère.

APPENDIX 5.

Transcript of draft letter from King Oscar II to Leopold II of Belgium, dated 4/1/1885. RA: UD 1902, Vol 4617 b.

Concept på egenhändigt svar på Konung Leopolds bref af den 23 December 1884. Dateradt Stockholm den 4 Januari 1885.

Sire! V.M. a bien voulu me faire part de son désir que les Royaumes Unis de S. et N. reconnaissent tout comme l'ont déjà fait l'Allemagne, l'Angleterre, l'Espagne les Etats Unis etc. le pavillon de l'Association International du Congo comme celui d'un état Ami.

Je m'empresse d'autant plus volontiers de répondre affirmativement à cette demande dont Elle m'a honoré, que j'y trouve une occasion nouvelle et bienvenue de pouvoir être agréable à V.M., dont l'œuvre civilisatrice poursuivie par Elle avec une persévérance si admirable et ci éclairée Lui a conquis les suffrages du monde entier. Le témoignage flatteur V.M. a en la bonté S'exprimer pour mes Officiers m'a fait grand plaisir et j'espère qu'ils s'en rendront dignes également à l'avenir. En servant V.M. ils savent bien qu'ils servent la cause de l'humanité. Ils s'en glorifient et avec raison.

J'attacherai toujours le plus grand prix à prouver par des actes la sympathie que je ressens pour la grande entreprise si chère à votre cœur, d'autant plus que j'y trouverai une occasion bien précieuse pour moi de témoigner à V.M. combien sont sincères les sentiments des constants amitié et de sympathie toute particulière avec lesquels je suis toujours.

Sire,
de V.M.
le bon Frère

O-2

CURRENT AFRICAN ISSUES PUBLISHED BY THE INSTITUTE
Recent issues in the series are available electronically
for download free of charge www.nai.uu.se

1981
1. *South Africa, the West and the Frontline States. Report from a Seminar.*
2. Maja Naur, *Social and Organisational Change in Libya.*
3. *Peasants and Agricultural Production in Africa. A Nordic Research Seminar. Follow-up Reports and Discussions.*

1985
4. Ray Bush & S. Kibble, *Destabilisation in Southern Africa, an Overview.*
5. Bertil Egerö, *Mozambique and the Southern African Struggle for Liberation.*

1986
6. Carol B.Thompson, *Regional Economic Polic under Crisis Condition. Southern African Development.*

1989
7. Inge Tvedten, *The War in Angola, Internal Conditions for Peace and Recovery.*
8. Patrick Wilmot, *Nigeria's Southern Africa Policy 1960–1988.*

1990
9. Jonathan Baker, *Perestroika for Ethiopia: In Search of the End of the Rainbow?*
10. Horace Campbell, *The Siege of Cuito Cuanavale.*

1991
11. Maria Bongartz, *The Civil War in Somalia. Its genesis and dynamics.*
12. Shadrack B.O. Gutto, *Human and People's Rights in Africa. Myths, Realities and Prospects.*
13. Said Chikhi, *Algeria. From Mass Rebellion to Workers' Protest.*
14. Bertil Odén, *Namibia's Economic Links to South Africa.*

1992
15. Cervenka Zdenek, *African National Congress Meets Eastern Europe. A Dialogue on Common Experiences.*

1993
16. Diallo Garba, *Mauritania–The Other Apartheid?*

1994
17. Zdenek Cervenka and Colin Legum, *Can National Dialogue Break the Power of Terror in Burundi?*
18. Erik Nordberg and Uno Winblad, *Urban Environmental Health and Hygiene in Sub-Saharan Africa.*

1996
19. Chris Dunton and Mai Palmberg, *Human Rights and Homosexuality in Southern Africa.*

1998
20. Georges Nzongola-Ntalaja, *From Zaire to the Democratic Republic of the Congo.*

1999
21. Filip Reyntjens, *Talking or Fighting? Political Evolution in Rwanda and Burundi, 1998–1999.*
22. Herbert Weiss, *War and Peace in the Democratic Republic of the Congo.*

2000
23. Filip Reyntjens, *Small States in an Unstable Region – Rwanda and Burundi, 1999–2000.*

2001
24. Filip Reyntjens, *Again at the Crossroads: Rwanda and Burundi, 2000–2001.*
25. Henning Melber, *The New African Initiative and the African Union. A Preliminary Assessment and Documentation.*

2003
26. Dahilon Yassin Mohamoda, *Nile Basin Cooperation. A Review of the Literature.*

2004
27. Henning Melber (ed.), *Media, Public Discourse and Political Contestation in Zimbabwe.*

28. Georges Nzongola-Ntalaja, *From Zaire to the Democratic Republic of the Congo.* (Second and Revised Edition)

2005

29. Henning Melber (ed.), *Trade, Development, Cooperation – What Future for Africa?*
30. Kaniye S.A. Ebeku, *The Succession of Faure Gnassingbe to the Togolese Presidency – An International Law Perspective.*
31. J.V. Lazarus, C. Christiansen, L. Rosendal Østergaard, L.A. Richey, Models for Life – Advancing antiretroviral therapy in sub-Saharan Africa.

2006

32. Charles Manga Fombad & Zein Kebonang, *AU, NEPAD and the APRM – Democratisation Efforts Explored.* (Ed. H. Melber.)
33. P.P. Leite, C. Olsson, M. Schöldtz, T. Shelley, P. Wrange, H. Corell and K. Scheele, *The Western Sahara Conflict – The Role of Natural Resources in Decolonization.* (Ed. Claes Olsson)

2007

34. Jassey, Katja and Stella Nyanzi, *How to Be a "Proper" Woman in the Times of HIV and AIDS.*
35. M. Lee, H. Melber, S. Naidu and I. Taylor, *China in Africa.* (Compiled by Henning Melber)
36. Nathaniel King, *Conflict as Integration. Youth Aspiration to Personhood in the Teleology of Sierra Leone's 'Senseless War'.*

2008

37. Aderanti Adepoju, *Migration in sub-Saharan Africa.*
38. Bo Malmberg, *Demography and the development potential of sub-Saharan Africa.*
39. Johan Holmberg, *Natural resources in sub-Saharan Africa: Assets and vulnerabilities.*
40. Arne Bigsten and Dick Durevall, *The African economy and its role in the world economy.*

41. Fantu Cheru, *Africa's development in the 21st century: Reshaping the research agenda.*

2009

42. Dan Kuwali, *Persuasive Prevention. Towards a Principle for Implementing Article 4(h) and R2P by the African Union.*
43. Daniel Volman, *China, India, Russia and the United States. The Scramble for African Oil and the Militarization of the Continent.*

2010

44. Mats Hårsmar, *Understanding Poverty in Africa? A Navigation through Disputed Concepts, Data and Terrains.*

2011

45. Sam Maghimbi, Razack B. Lokina and Mathew A. Senga, *The Agrarian Question in Tanzania? A State of the Art Paper.*
46. William Minter, *African Migration, Global Inequalities, and Human Rights. Connecting the Dots.*
47. Musa Abutudu and Dauda Garuba, *Natural Resource Governance and EITI Implementation in Nigeria.*
48. Ilda Lindell, *Transnational Activism Networks and Gendered Gatekeeping. Negotiating Gender in an African Association of Informal Workers.*

2012

49. Terje Oestigaard, *Water Scarcity and Food Security along the Nile. Politics, population increase and climate change.*
50. David Ross Olanya, *From Global Land Grabbing for Biofuels to Acquisitions of AfricanWater for Commercial Agriculture.*

2013

51. Gessesse Dessie, *Favouring a Demonised Plant. Khat and Ethiopian smallholder enterprise.*
52. Boima Tucker, *Musical Violence. Gangsta Rap and Politics in Sierra Leone.*
53. David Nilsson, *Sweden-Norway at the Berlin Conference 1884–85. History, national identity-making and Sweden's relations with Africa*

www.ingramcontent.com/pod-product-compliance
Ingram Content Group UK Ltd.
Pitfield, Milton Keynes, MK11 3LW, UK
UKHW051652180426
11947UKWH00021B/1913